JERUSA

CALIPHATE

AND THE

THIRD JIHAD

JOHN C. WITCOMBE

PROPHECY WAYMARKS PUBLICATIONS
HELENA, MONTANA

Page layout by Page One Communications

Cover design by Lars Justinen–Justinen Creative Group

Cover image: Jerusalem at Night–© Depositphotos Inc.

Cover image: Islam Will Dominate the World–© TC & Reve Ltd.

Library of Congress Control Number: 2013918859

Contact the author by visiting: JerusalemCaliphate.com

Also available in e-book format

ISBN: 978-0-9911047-0-3

CONTENTS

A NOTE FROM
THE AUTHOR

Books on the Middle East crisis are proliferating like baby rabbits these days! With such a selection available, why should you invest your time in reading this book? If the cover title didn't spark an interest, perhaps I need to speak plainer: If I lived in Israel today, and if I didn't want to live under Islamic Sharia law, I would put my house on the market and "get out of Dodge." Why? Daniel 11:45 is why—*"And he shall plant the tabernacles of his palace between the seas in the glorious holy mountain. . ."*

Based upon a reasonable interpretation of this prophecy, this book is proposing that the leader of Turkey is going to plant a restored caliphate[1] on the Mount of Olives overlooking the Dome of the Rock in Jerusalem. Yes, I know this is a pretty bold proposition to be making; but the evidence presented in this book is *absolutely* compelling.

And if you don't live in Israel? The aftermath of what is soon to take place there will affect those who live in Western societies. A Third Jihad will especially target Western countries with the same intensity that history reports of the first two Jihads. The tragedy of 9/11 will seem mild in comparison to what is coming.

This book will present a view of the near future that you probably have never heard before, yet it was widely taught in the nineteenth century. I have in my possession an old, leather-bound, 1891 edition of *Daniel and the Revelation* that I bought on eBay for $60. This musty 854-page book is a verse-by-verse commentary on the two apocalyptic books of the Bible. A best seller, it has sold close to a million copies in multiple languages.

In 2010, I read the author's interpretation of Daniel 11:45 and immediately saw its relevance to what was happening in our world today. The

---

1. A caliphate is the religio-political governance of the caliph, who rules under Islamic law (Sharia). The caliph is the head of the *ummah*—the Muslim community throughout the world.

author of *Daniel and the Revelation* had applied his interpretation of this verse to the geopolitical conditions of his day. I simply updated his application to reflect the geopolitical landscape of our day and saw that we were on the verge of a stupendous crisis.

Even without the benefit of Bible prophecy, one could simply look at what is happening today and be able to forecast such a scenario as this book will lay out. But after a careful examination of the 11th chapter of Daniel, I believe that you too will clearly see the future as portended by the title of this book—*Jerusalem Caliphate and the Third Jihad.*

John Witcombe

Note: Much in the Islamic world has transpired since this book was first published in 2013. Top Arab media outlets recognize the significance of what took place in the referendum vote in Turkey on April 16, 2017. In a headline titled, "Finally Erdogan succeeded in transforming Turkey into the New Ottoman Caliphate", Al-Dehi writes:

> "Will NATO now be silent on Turkey? The Referendum now transforms Erdogan into a semi-god. This achievement is the formation of the Ottoman caliphate. Turkey now will enter a dark tunnel. There is a great division within Turkish society and Erdogan's success will make him avenge the Kurds and the nationalists. It is the end of Ataturkism and the beginning of the Erdoganian Caliphate." https://www.elbalad.news/2720966

For the latest news and information regarding the prophecies dealt with in this book, go to **JerusalemCaliphate.com** and click on the NEWS tab.

INTRODUCTION

On that fateful September morning in 2001 when the Twin Towers in New York City were attacked and destroyed, the attention of the Western world was suddenly focused on unfamiliar words: *terrorism, Al Qaeda,* and even *Islam.*

In the years since, awareness of the goals of a determined Islamic world has grown—though even today, many in the West do not fully understand the plans Islam has for the world. While we in the Americas and Europe go about our busy lives, preoccupied with our daily pursuits and concerns—family and relationships, career, health, finances, entertainment—many in the Muslim world focus largely on the single-minded goal of bringing the entire world under the dominion of Islam.

"Islam wishes to destroy all States and Governments anywhere on the face of the earth which are opposed to the ideology and programme of Islam regardless of the country or the Nation that rules it. Islam requires the earth—not just a portion—but the whole planet." *Jihad in Islam*, by deceased Islamic scholar Sayyid Abul Ala Maududi.

Maududi was an influential Pakistani journalist, theologian and Muslim revivalist leader, who wrote more than 120 books and pamphlets. He lived from 1903 to 1979 and is described in the preface of one of the books as an author who "provided the present-day revival of Islam with its intellectual foundations."[1]

Few understand just what is going on "under the radar" of their awareness. Fewer still understand the level of commitment Islam—the world's second-largest and, by some measures, its fastest-growing religion—brings to its mission of global dominance.

---

1.   <http://www.israelnationalnews.com/News/News.aspx/154434#.Uktb-HoZwqY1>.

The book you hold in your hands is unique and has two goals. First, in these pages, the author will present Islam's rise in history, its present efforts to achieve its ends, and its plans to unite the world under Islamic Sharia law.

In presenting these facts, this book will necessarily speak to the "three Jihads"—times of epic struggle and expansion of Islam through largely military conquest. History is witness that these Jihads (two in the past) were militant, violent, and resulted in millions of deaths. A future third and final Jihad is likely to be no different in this respect.

But to acknowledge that Islam has been, is, and will continue to use militant and violent means to its ends is not—and this point is vital—to characterize all Islam as composed only of those who believe in and use violence. Many individual Muslims are as peace-loving as those to be found in many other religions. Just as historically, the Roman Catholic Church, too, has employed violence in pursuit of its goals, yet is today composed overwhelmingly of devout and peace-loving members, the same is true of Islam.

So it is important to note the great difference between the *system* of Islam and the character of many of its members.

A second goal of this book will be to present startling prophetic information from the Bible concerning the rise of Islam, its role in the final events of this world's history, and the prophetic significance of Islam's three Jihads in fulfilling the three "woes" of Bible prophecy found in the book of Revelation.

The hope of this book's author is that those of all faiths will be intrigued by the information presented here—information found nowhere else in print, to date. Especially is it hoped that Muslims will be impressed with the importance of the role they have played—and are about to play—in world events and in the fulfillment of the Christian Scriptures, the Bible.

God has used Islam in times past to visit redemptive discipline on nations supporting apostate religions. And today, especially in the West, much of contemporary Christianity is in a state of rebellious compromise on a wide range of issues. Could God be ready to work through Islam once again to bring His discipline on those nations supporting compromised Christianity?

Whether you are of Islam, Christianity, Judaism, Buddhism, Hinduism, Atheism, any other religion, or no religion at all, this book is an invitation to go behind the headlines to learn the truth of what is quietly building toward a mighty, final clash of the world's competing civilizations. It's an eye-opening wake-up call to become informed, ahead of time, as to what will soon dominate every news cycle, every headline, every family and neighborhood conversation.

Jerusalem Caliphate and the Third Jihad is your window into a very real and soon-coming global fight for world domination. And with that, let chapter 1 begin!

CHAPTER ONE

THE FINAL JIHAD

"The peak, the pinnacle, the quest, the highest point, the pivot, the summit of Islam is...Jihad."
—Sheik Feiz Mohammad, Head, Global Islamic Youth Center

Jihad.

To many of us in the Western world, *Jihad* is just another of those strange-sounding words from the world of Islam that have slowly found their way into our consciousness—especially since 9/11. Words such as *mujahedeen, intifada, caliphate, fatwa, Ramadan, Taliban, Sunnis and Shiites, Al Qaeda,* or *Sharia.*

But what is the meaning of *Jihad?*[1]

And why refer to one Jihad as "final"?

The Islamic word *Jihad* means "struggle." And for Muslims, that

---

1.   The influential *Dictionary of Islam* defines Jihad as *"A religious war with those who are unbelievers in the mission of Muhammad. It is an incumbent religious duty, established in the Qur'an and in the Traditions as a divine institution, and enjoined specially for the purpose of advancing Islam and of repelling evil from Muslims....* [quoting from the Hanafi school, Hedaya, 2:140, 141] *The destruction of the sword is incurred by infidels, although they be not the first aggressors, as appears from various passages in the traditions which are generally received to this effect."*—Thomas Patrick Hughes (London: W. H. Allen & Co., 1895).

can mean either the inner, personal struggle to fulfill one's religious duties—or the outer, physical struggle against the enemies of Islam, to whom Muslims often refer as *infidels*. This outer struggle can be either violent or non-violent. Those who emphasize the violent struggle refer to it as "holy war"—usually military in its execution.

History records two great Jihads, during which Islam expanded rapidly and largely through military conquests. A primary and urgent theme of this book is that *a prophesied third and final Jihad is imminent.* Each of these Jihads will be addressed in more detail in later chapters, but in brief, here is an overview of the three Jihads.

The First Jihad

Islam's first Jihad[2] took place as its founding prophet Muhammad sent his armies to conquer Arabia, beginning in A.D. 622. After Muhammad's death in A.D. 632, this Jihad continued more than another hundred years until A.D. 750. Muhammad was succeeded by a series of leaders known as *Caliphs:* Abu Bakr, Umar, Uthman, Ali, and other Caliphs, who led out in this first great Jihad, or expansion of Islam.

After conquering Arabia, the Islamic armies—with the surprising swiftness of a blitzkrieg—swept into the Holy Land, including also Iraq and Iran, then pushed west across North Africa and on into Spain and France. The eastern advance of this first Jihad reached deep into Central Asia.

The Second Jihad

A second major Jihad[3] took place between A.D. 1071 and A.D. 1683. A key victory in this Jihad was the taking of the Christian capital of Constantinople in A.D. 1453. Muslim armies pushed into Europe from the southeast—all the way to Austria. They expanded their reach deeper into North Africa and in the east, into India. Untold millions—Africans, Arabs, Christians, Hindus, Buddhists, and Jews—were killed in these first two Jihads.

The Third Jihad

Many believe that the early actions of a third and final Jihad[4] are already underway. Others consider these aggressions—including such

---

2.   <http://www.jihadwatch.org/islam-101.html>; <http://www.peacewithrealism.org/jihad/jihad05.htm>.

3.   <http://www.jihadwatch.org/islam-101.html>.

4.   <http://www.thethirdjihad.com/>.

attacks as 9/11 and the bombings of the U.S.S. *Cole*, Madrid subway, and Pan Am Flight 103—as relatively minor actions preceding an imminent third Jihad.

Either way, it is clear from the stated intentions of Islamic leaders that a third Jihad—with the goal of bringing the entire world under the dominance of Islam—is inevitable. Nothing less than subjugating all other religions and leaving not an inch of global soil where Islam is not in control, will be acceptable to those who understand the teachings of the Quran regarding the destiny of Islam.

Wake-Up Call

Most of us in the western world live largely unaware of the growing tide of Islam in the world—and of its commitment to bring the entire world under the rule of Islamic law.

We're busy, after all. Our time and attention is focused on our own daily routines: work and careers, family and friendships, the ongoing struggle to make ends meet financially, and all the other insistent claims of our "To Do" lists. We have little time or occasion to reflect on what's happening on the other side of the world—or even focus much on the inroads of Islam right here in our own backyards.

Islam—the world's second-largest religion and by some measures, its fastest-growing—forges far ahead of Christianity in its growth rate. If the rates of these two leading religions were to continue unchanged, it would not be all that long before they exchanged places, with Islam surpassing Christianity to become the globe's largest religion.

Preoccupied with our own lives, we who live as Christians, atheists, Hindus, Buddhists, members of the Jewish faith, or no faith at all, have become complacent, apathetic, largely unaware of what is—by the statements of Islamic leaders themselves—shaping up to be an enormous threat to our way of life and our beliefs.

Only when an occasional disastrous event, such as 9/11 or, say, the Boston marathon bombings, captures the headlines, do we note that Jihadis have not been sleeping and are plotting constantly to bring death and destruction to the western world. Only through vigilant efforts have we already (to date, at least) been spared the destruction of Chicago's Sears Tower, deadly subway attacks, and others.

Is this book the little boy who cried "Wolf!"? Is it Chicken Little, warning that "the sky is falling!"? Perhaps one way to form a conclusion as to these questions is to survey a few of the pertinent comments from the leaders of Islam themselves. What are *they* saying?

> *"We will conquer the world, for the victory of [Islam's] saying, 'There is no God but Allah, and Muhammad is Allah's messenger, over the domes of Moscow, Washington, and Paris."*— Ayatollah Ahmad Husseini Al-Baghdadi.

> *"In the Jihad which you are seeking, you look for the enemy and invade him. This type of Jihad takes place only when the Islamic state is invading other* [countries] *in order to spread the word of Islam and to remove obstacles standing in its way.... Islam has the right to take the initiative...this is God's religion and it is for the whole world. It has the right to destroy all obstacles in the form of institutions and traditions...it attacks institutions and traditions to release human beings from their poisonous influences, which distort human nature and curtail human freedom. Those who say that Islamic Jihad was merely for the defense of the 'homeland of Islam' diminish the greatness of the Islamic way of life."*—Sheikh Yusuf al-Qaradawi (one of Islam's most revered modern scholars).

> *"The holy war is a religious duty, because of the universalism of the Muslim mission and (the obligation to) convert everybody to Islam either by persuasion or by force"*—Ibn Khaldun (one of Islam's most respected philosophers).

Cultural Jihad

Particularly in parts of the world such as the West, where Islam is not the dominant religion, the battle of ideologies is carried out less by military and violent means, than by steady infiltration of the societal culture. But make no mistake—the goals of Islam remain unchanged:

A 15-page document known as the *Manifesto of Muslim Brotherhood in North America* says this on page 7: *"Grand Jihad is eliminating and destroying the Western civilization from within."* The stated goal is for *"Allah's religion to be made victorious over all other religions."*

> *"Before Allah closes our eyes for the last time, you will see Islam move from being the second-largest religion in America—that's where we are now—to being the first religion in America."*—Imam Johari Abdul Malik, Chairman, coordinating Council of Muslim Organizations.

One of the more effective means of infiltrating Western society and "winning from within" is the growing effort to enlist the minds and hearts of those in prison. In New York State, for example, an estimated 18 percent of inmates are now Muslims. Contributing to this result are the recruiting activities of Islamic prison chaplains. Consider the words of a former chaplain in the New York City Corrections Department to inmates:

"Brothers, be prepared to fight, be prepared to die, be prepared to kill. It's a part of the faith, and this ain't your brother just saying this. This is history, this is Koran, nobody can deny it...When you fight, you strike terror into the heart of the disbeliever."—Warith Deen Umar, Former Chaplain, NYC Corrections Department.

And once released, many ex-prisoners are urged to join Jihadist training centers such as "Islamberg" in upstate New York, one of at least 30 such known compounds in the U.S. Here, videos have surfaced showing training in use of various weapons, as well as bomb-making. Many of these centers are operated by Sheikh Gilani, head of the Al Fuqra Movement out of Pakistan, with links to a number of Jihadist activities.

The Nuclear Threat

Of course, the threat most feared is that nuclear devices will find their way, either into the hands of militant Islamic groups or a Muslim-dominant state such as Iran. Many suspect that Iran is very close to being nuclear-capable—and that once that point is reached, Iran will not hesitate to use such weapons.

The old "Cold War" deterrent—M.A.D., or Mutually Assured Destruction—no longer applies to Islamic groups or countries, since they would have no hesitation to pay the price of their own destruction to assure the destruction of their enemies. After all, Allah knows his own, as they see it—and he can sort out any casualties and give a swift pass to paradise for those "martyred" in a possible nuclear war.

These days, a nuclear device with power comparable to the one which destroyed Hiroshima can fit into a suitcase. And one level down from nuclear devices in destructive power are so-called "dirty bombs," which could use a smaller nuclear charge to spread deadly chemical or biological agents to destroy tens of thousands.

Restoration of the Caliphate: Whither Islam?

Before Islam can be fully prepared to reassert its march to global dominance, however, the disparate and fragmented factions of Islam must somehow be united under a single Muslim leader—a system that prevailed through centuries until the year 1924. That leader was known as the *Caliph,* and the system of governance known as a *Caliphate.*

Consider now a former Fox News commentator known for his long and sometimes emotional rants on politically oriented topics, who picks up the idea of a restored Islamic caliphate and runs with it. Islam, he says, is gearing up to set up a unified Islamic government intent on nothing short of world domination.

Critics—enough to fill a Super Bowl stadium—call him a loon. A conspiracy nutjob. A blathering idiot.

Let's grant that network pundits aren't Bible prophets with inside information on what's coming. And sensationalism is the stuff of ratings, so no surprise that the theories of these "talking heads" are so often viewed with a jaundiced eye or are considered laughable. Besides, in this increasingly fractured world of ours, Pied Pipers of every extremist persuasion find hordes of the gullible willing to part with their own common sense and follow them to the fringes or even to ultimate destruction. Jim Jones or David Koresh, anyone?

All of this said, a question remains: Under the layers of fearmongering, the hype and hysteria the media employs to pump up their viewer numbers—and in spite of the confusion and contradictions of their so-called predictions—is a startling truth lurking there that we dismiss at our peril? For example, does the ancient Good Book itself have anything to say about the growing power and influence of Islam that's now a part of every day's news? Does Christianity's Bible even suggest or allow for such a seemingly outlandish idea as the restoration of an Islamic caliphate?

Speaking of which, what *IS* a caliphate? Put most simply, *caliphate* derives from the Arabic name (*khilãfa*) for the first system of government in Islam—and the *caliph* was the head of state and religious leader. Initially, the caliphate was formed by the disciples of Muhammad as a continuation of the religio-political system the prophet himself established.

The first Islamic caliph was Abu Bakr, Muhammad's father-in-law, who ruled from A.D. 632–634, after the prophet's death. The caliphate continued through the centuries until 1924, when, on March 3, Mustafa Kemal Atatürk, the first president of the Turkish Republic, constitutionally abolished the office of the caliphate.

Today, from many quarters of Islam arise calls for the restoration of the caliphate—for the uniting of Islam under one centralized government and ruler. Is this goal preposterous? Impossible? Should such calls be regarded as idle Islamic pipe dreams? Or is this a rock-solid determination?

We need to get this right.

Consider and reflect: Have we ever "gotten it wrong" before as a nation? Have we ever not listened—miscalculated, underestimated, *assumed?*

Did we have chances to know Pearl Harbor was about to happen? Did hubris lead us to think our superior firepower could make quick work of Vietnam? Was 9/11 really a surprise, after all the outright warnings it was imminent? Wasn't the eventual imbroglio of Iraq supposed to be over within days of "shock and awe"?

And what about today? Are we really *listening* to what many of Islam's religious leaders are saying?

When they say that their goal is to unite the world under Islam as the one and only world religion—do we dismiss or excuse or ignore or minimize their words and refuse to take them seriously? Have their actions to date corresponded to their words—or not?

Before Pearl Harbor, before Vietnam, before 9/11, before Iraq—and many other times in our history—we have perhaps too often responded to those bearing warnings beforehand, either by ignoring them or deriding them. We've called them fear-mongers, panic peddlers, conspiracy merchants.

Now, make no mistake. We live in a world riddled with every kind of fear—both real and imagined. We live in a society that gets its daily adrenaline rush from the scary and the sensational. And the chosen and profitable enterprise of the media is to fuel that fear, stoke the sensational, and perpetuate the panic. And without doubt, the great majority of this fear-hyped hysteria is utterly artificial. But the worlds of marketing and media know the motivating power of fear. They know that they can make enormous profits when people are afraid. People will pay almost anything to be safe. Raise the specter of insecurity, and there's money to be made. Make people afraid, and controlling them becomes quite easy.

And government knows it can increase its control over the lives of its citizens by citing "national security" as the justification for steadily stripping away basic civil, human, and even constitutional rights. Thus, the Department of Homeland SECURITY; the Transportation SECURITY Administration.

But just because so much of the fear and panic and conspiracy theorizing abounding today is artificially induced—and just because some TV talking heads are indeed trafficking in far-fetched fantasies—that does not mean we can safely dismiss or discount *all* warnings, even some of theirs. Perhaps even in the most over-the-top rantings may be found a core, a kernel, of truth and reality.

If a pundit or politician tells us to be afraid, very afraid, of militant Islam, we may consider the source and decide nothing he says is to be trusted.

But what if, in that warning that the sky is falling, one important truth can be found? And if so, how can we ever know—between the truth and the sensational—which is which?

It's not that hard. Listen to the *original* source, or sources. We may wisely be skeptical of what others report or opine that we should fear. But if, perhaps with reason, we may doubt the credibility of, say, a pundit or politician or journalist who warns of the goals of Islam, what of those Islamic sources themselves? What do *they* say? And even more important, what—for those with confidence in the Bible's prophets—do *they* say?

Yes, about the agenda and veracity of the media's second- or third-hand fear-mongering, we may well have heavy reservations, but what about first-hand sources? Read these recent words—then decide for yourself whether these speakers mean what they say. Decide whether they are overdramatizing just for effect, or are stating with unshakeable determination what they fully intend to do:

Excerpts from an address by Hamas MP and cleric Yunis Al-Astal, on Al-Aqsa TV, May 11, 2011:

> "The [Jews] are brought in droves to Palestine so that the Palestinians—and the Islamic nation behind them—will have the honor of annihilating the evil of this gang....

> "All the predators, all the birds of prey, all the dangerous reptiles and insects, and all the lethal bacteria are far less dangerous than the Jews....

> "In just a few years, all the Zionists and the settlers will realize that their arrival in Palestine was for the purpose of the great massacre, by means of which Allah wants to relieve humanity of their evil....

> "When Palestine is liberated and its people return to it, and the entire region, with the grace of Allah, will have turned into the

United States of Islam, the land of Palestine will become the capital of the Islamic Caliphate, and all these countries will turn into states within the Caliphate."

Statements aired on Al-Aqsa TV on November 3, 2011, at a rally of the pro-Hamas Palestinian Al-Ahrar movement in Gaza. Rally organizer:

"Praise be to you, our Lord. You have made our killing of the Jews an act of worship, through which we come closer to you....

"Allah's prayers upon you, our beloved Prophet [Muhammad]. You have made your teachings into constitutions for us—the light with which we dissipate the darkness of the occupation, and the fire with which we harvest the skulls of the Jews....

"Yes, our beloved brothers, even though the entire world moves closer to Allah through fasting, through hunger, and through tears, we are a people that moves closer to Allah through blood, through body parts, and through martyrs....

"Oh sons of Palestine, oh sons of the Gaza Strip, oh Mujahideen—wage Jihad, wreak destruction, blow up and harvest the heads of the Zionists. Words are useless by now. The lie of peace is gone. Only weapons are of any use—the path of [recently killed] Yousuf and Ali, the path of martyrdom and Jihad. Only our wounds talk on our behalf. We speak nothing but the language of struggle, of Jihad, [of] rockets, of bombs, of cannons and of martyrdom-seekers. This is the language in which we talk and negotiate with the Zionist enemy...

"We say to the Zionists: Like a bad seed, we shall uproot you from our land, so that it can blossom in the light of the everlasting sun of our Jihad, and of our invincible religion. Jerusalem is not yours—get out of it! Haifa is not yours—get out of it! Tel Aviv is not yours—get out of it! Oh Zionists, get out before we expel you. These are the words of the Mujahideen."

Egyptian Shaykh Safwat Hegazy, member of the Muslim Brotherhood, in a video posted to YouTube on October 2, 2009:

"I say unto you that we will return. Jerusalem belongs to us. Al-Aqsa belongs to us. Jerusalem belongs to us, and the whole world belongs to us. Every land upon which Islam has set foot will return to us. The caliphate will return to us, on the platform of prophecy. The greatness and glory of Islam will return."

Plain enough?

"Oh," some will protest, "but those are only isolated voices. Those are just the extremists or militants of Islam talking. The great majority of Islam is made up of peace-loving members who reject this kind of talk."

Can we be so sure of that?

To paint any group—especially any religion—with the same broad brush would be reprehensible and unfair. To conclude that all followers of Muhammad seek war and destruction would be an enormous and egregious mistake. Many of the world's 1.57 billion Muslims live peacefully and desire peace just as much as most Christians and Jews do.

But as is so true of any organized group of humans—political, religious, organizational, or institutional—leaders lead, and followers follow. And without question, today's Muslim leaders seek a restoration of their authority—the unity of all Islam and ultimately, the world, under one faith, centered in one place.

If any doubt that entire populations can be manipulated or forced by extremist leaders into going along with an evil agenda, simply remember the Holocaust.

Many readers will have lived long enough to remember a time when Islam was barely known or spoken of—at least here in the United States. Some of us remember a time when the unceasing conflicts of man centered on the world wars—first and second. Then came the interlude of the Cold War—a frightening standoff between the world's two great superpowers.

Barely had the Soviet Union collapsed, than World Wars and the Cold War were abruptly replaced by a whole new kind of war—the War on Terror. And surging with it into the public consciousness came the heretofore little-known agenda and tactics of Islam.

The time will never come when Islam will simply recede till it once again barely registers in our collective consciousness. Islam is here to stay. The onward march of Islam is rapid and relentless. Its presence and agenda are not to be ignored. And woe be to any who choose to minimize or deride its words or underestimate its intentions.

At least that isn't a mistake America's government seems likely to make. The possibility of a restored Islamic caliphate is an acknowledged part of its foreign policy calculations. In the following statement, perhaps like the author, you too will note the irony of a nation that routinely employs fear for its own ends, yet which itself often operates out of fear:

"Despite the Obama administration's abandonment of the phrase 'war on terror,' the impulses encoded in it still powerfully shape Washington's policy-making, as well as its geopolitical fears and fantasies. It adds up to an absurdly modernized version of domino theory. *This irrational fear that any small setback for the U.S. in the Muslim world could lead straight to an Islamic caliphate lurks beneath many of Washington's pronouncements and much of its strategic planning.*"—Juan Cole, CBSNews.com, January 28, 2011 (originally in TomDispatch.com, January 25, 2011), emphasis supplied.

History and current events tell us much about the growing impact of Islam in our world. But this book has a larger intent than simply to review Islam's past and describe its present. Guided by the light of ancient Bible prophets, it seeks to preview its future. To uncritically accept the tabloid-ish predictions of media commentators is one thing. To place confidence and hope and credence in the words of prophets such as Daniel and his eponymously named Old Testament book—and John, who wrote the New Testament's book of Revelation—is quite another.

The focus of this book will be especially on a single chapter of the book of Daniel. And even more so, on a single verse of that chapter. For in those words, for those who "have ears to hear," is found an ancient message that outlines the role of the Mideast and a resurgent Islam, both now and in the world's final days, just ahead.

Can anyone know with precision and detail just how even the Bible's prophecies will unfold, when they actually come to pass? Can we combine those prophecies with the unequivocally stated goals of today's militant Islam and then describe with certainty what is about to happen in our world?

No. No more than we can know perfectly *anything* that hasn't yet occurred.

But the author of this book is convinced that the Bible's track record on prophecy is 100 percent, and that it is not illegitimate and wild speculation to imagine a scenario that begins with what Bible prophecy makes certain—and builds on those known details.

So before beginning a careful look at the Bible's books of Daniel and Revelation—and what they may have to suggest to us about Islam and its growing role in the world—consider the possibility of an Islamic world newly united under the leadership of a restored caliphate. Since the ending of the caliphate in 1924, Islam has largely lost the strength that always resides in unity. The various factions of Islam have ever since often worked at cross-purposes with each other.

But what could happen were a single caliph to unite Islam from his headquarters in the Holy Land? And could that take place sooner than most could ever imagine?

CHAPTER TWO

RESTORATION OF THE CALIPHATE

- **Osama bin Laden** envisioned it: The entire world united under a restored Islamic caliphate, ruled by Sharia law.

- **Taliban** commander Omar Khalid al Khurasani has said: "Until Islam is implemented in Pakistan and Afghanistan, and the Caliphate is established across the world, our jihad will continue. This is our first and foremost objective."

- **Al Qaeda** has the restoration of the caliphate as its ultimate goal. They have named their Internet newscast "The Voice of the Caliphate."

- **The Muslim Brotherhood**—founded in 1928 by Egyptian schoolteacher Hassan al Banna, just four years after abolition of the caliphate, is now one of the largest and most influential Islamic organizations and has stated its ultimate goal as reestablishing the caliphate in pursuit of Islamic "mastership of the world."

- **Hamas**—an outgrowth of the Muslim Brotherhood located in Palestine—holds to the ultimate Islamic goal of a restored caliphate, along with ultimate destruction of Israel and reoccupation of Israeli territory.

- **Hezbollah**—based in Lebanon—aims for a restored caliphate.

- **Hizb ut-Tahrir** rivals the Muslim Brotherhood in size and influence in the Islamic world and as one of the most committed organizations to the goal of a restored caliphate, has drafted a provisional constitution for a modern caliph-led, Sharia-ruled, pan-Islamic state.

▶ **A recent poll** showed that more than two thirds of people in four Muslim nations say they support the idea of unifying all Muslim countries in "a single Islamic state or caliphate."

Caliphate, as noted in the previous chapter, is an Arabic word (from *khilāfa*) referring to an Islamic state ruled by a *caliph*—a word meaning "successor" (of the founding prophet Muhammad)—a supreme religious and political leader unifying Islam under the rule of Sharia law.

Since the caliphate abruptly ended in 1924 with the end of the Ottoman (Turkish) Empire, the Islamic dream of a restored caliphate has continued, becoming increasingly a common aim of virtually all factions and organizations of Islam.

From the first caliph, Abu Bakr—who succeeded Muhammad upon the prophet's death in A.D. 632, to the last caliph, Abdülmecid II, who was deposed by Turkey's first president, Mustafa Kemal Atatürk, on March 3, 1924—the caliphate was Islam's system of governance. Along the way were some "bumps in the road (rival caliphs, for example), but the system survived for nearly 1,300 years. From the mid-1500s onward, the office of caliph in the Ottoman Empire—till then primarily a religious one—became also a more political office, often combining the titles of caliph and *sultan.*

Brief History of the Caliphate

The first four caliphs to lead Islam following Muhammad's death in A.D. 632 were: Abu Bakr as-Siddiq, Umah ibn al-Khattab, Uthman ibn Affan, and Ali ibn Abi Talib. Together, these four caliphs came to be known as the "rightly guided successors" of Muhammad, having been his close companions during his prophethood. Following these four, the caliphate continued through a succession of dynasties: the Umayyads (A.D. 661–750), the Abbasids (A.D. 750–1517), and the Ottomans (A.D. 1517–1924). Other competing dynasties (the Fatimids, the Rahmanids, the Almohads) were not universally accepted in Islam and ruled only parts of the Islamic world.

Perhaps the most notable of the historical caliphs was Suleiman I ("the Magnificent" and "the Lawgiver"—A.D. 1494–1566), whose titles included Caliph of Islam and Sultan of the Ottoman Empire. During his reign, the Ottoman Empire reached the zenith of its expansion, conquering most of the Middle East, North Africa, and forging well into Europe.

But by the early 1900s, the old Ottoman Empire was greatly weakened, contracted, and in decline. After World War I, Mustafa Kemal Atatürk (his surname, meaning "Father of the Turks," was granted him by the Turkish parliament), with the backing of the British government, led in establishing Turkey as a secular state, moving the capital from Constantinople (Istanbul) to Ankara. And on March 3, 1924, through the Turkish Grand National Assembly, he dissolved the office of the caliphate. The final caliph, Abdülmecid II, was deposed and sent into exile.

Expectations of a Restored Caliphate

Through the nine-tenths of a century since 1924, the dream of a re-established caliphate has for the majority of Muslims never gone away. Increasingly, from many corners of the Islamic world come calls for—reflecting expectations of—a restored caliphate. A few examples:

"The new era for the caliphate is on the way!"
—Shaykh Abdul Majeed al-Zindani, Yemen, March 2011.

"The Caliphate in the path of the Prophet will return.... The people want the restoration of the Caliphate."
—Jordanian Sheik Nader Tamimi, Mufti of the Palestine Liberation Army, on Memri TV (the Internet), December 15, 2011.

"We can see how the dream of the Islamic Caliphate is being realized, Allah willing.... We can see how the great dream, shared by us all—that of the United States of the Arabs—will be restored, Allah willing.... The capital of the Caliphate—the capital of the United States of the Arabs—will be Jerusalem, Allah willing.... Our capital shall not be Cairo, Mecca, or Medina. It shall be Jerusalem, Allah willing."
—Cleric Safwat Higazi, May 1, 2012, at a rally in support of then-candidate and eventual Egyptian president (since toppled) Mohamed Morsi (of the Muslim Brotherhood).

"Listen, Obama, the Caliphate will return...the Caliphate is the answer.... Listen, Obama, we are a nation that does not bow down, and the Caliphate will return!"
— Hizb ut-Tahrir Imam, speaking at the al-Aqsa Mosque in Jerusalem, July 12, 2013.

So from all across the Muslim world come ever-more-frequent calls for reestablishing the caliphate. And many outside the Islamic *ummah* (community) also voice expectations—or at least fears—of a restored caliphate, uniting a currently divided Muslim world into a cohesive, single-minded superstate (a "United Islamic States"?) bent on global domination under the worldwide rule of Sharia law.

Sharia Law

By the way, a word here before proceeding, on Sharia law. Considered the infallible law of Allah, Sharia is the moral and religious law of Islam. It addresses many topics of secular concern—politics, crime, economics—but also personal matters such as sexual behavior, hygiene, diet, prayer, and fasting.

Sharia has two primary sources. Primary are the precepts contained in the Quran, but second only to the Quran is the *Sunnah*—the teachings, practices, and example of the prophet Muhammed. The Sunnah includes his specific words, habits, practices, and even his silent approvals.

Sharia law is interpreted by Islamic judges (*qadis*) and by Islamic religious leaders (*imams*). For questions not directly answered in the Quran or Sunnah, religious scholars (*ulama*) reach a consensus on how to apply those primary sources of Sharia. Much of Sharia law is considered by non-Muslims to be excessively harsh.

A Battle of Brothers

A global caliphate imposing Sharia law on the entire world? Is that only a far-fetched fantasy? Do remember that even though divided in many ways, the Islamic world is becoming increasingly united in its determination to restore the caliphate as the key to unity—and to set the stage for a final, great Third Jihad.

Remember too that the Middle East is more unstable with every passing week. One errant missile, one rogue nation finally achieving nuclear capability, one radical faction, or even full nation, abruptly invading another sovereign territory—and the entire region could instantly be plunged into chaos. Can any of us really believe that such a prospect doesn't keep leaders in Washington, D.C. up at night? Do we really think that those who more frequently now publicly worry about falling into the abyss of World War III—a final Armageddon—are just fretting about nothing? After all, the Middle East is...

A tinderbox.

A landmine.

A live bomb.

For decades, the Middle East has simmered, as Israel and Arab nations cling to ancient hatreds. As ancient as Old Testament Abraham, from whose sons Isaac (Israel) and Ishmael (Arab nations) descended.

"And the angel of the LORD said unto her, Behold, thou art with child, and shalt bear a son, and shalt call his name Ishmael; because the LORD hath heard thy affliction. And he will be a wild man; his hand will be against every man, and every man's hand against him; and he shall dwell in the presence of all his brethren."—Genesis 16:11, 12.

"And as for Ishmael, I have heard thee: Behold, I have blessed him, and will make him fruitful, and will multiply him exceedingly; twelve princes shall he beget, and I will make him a great nation."—Genesis 17:20.

Both the descendants of Isaac and Ishmael trace their competing claims to land and divine favor to God's promises to Abraham.

In recent decades, the broader standoff between Israel and the entire Arab world has narrowed so that today, it's more between Israel and Palestine—as some Arab nations have signed uneasy peace accords with the Jewish state. But the entire area of the Middle East and North Africa remains a place of constant turmoil and threat—and with the increasing growth of Islam in the region, other Arab nations too share the ultimate goal of returning Jerusalem and all Israel to Arab-Islamic occupation and control.

Most recently, the focus has shifted to include not just Palestine as a most immediate threat to Israel but also to Iran. Both continue to deny that Israel as a nation even has a right to exist.

Iran: Until 1935 known as Persia—and since 1979 a theocratic Islamic republic of 78 million ruled by an Islamic Ayatollah known as the Supreme Leader. Subordinate to the Supreme Leader is Iran's president—though recent presidents have sometimes, but unsuccessfully, challenged the Islamic leader for control of the country.

Iran: A "loose cannon" nation at ease with using violence and terror to advance its vision of a world ultimately under the power of an Islamic caliphate.

Iran: A growing threat and concern both to Israel and all its Western allies, including the United States, because it continues defiantly to develop a nuclear weapons program. And it's unlikely Iran is doing so only to defend itself or use nuclear power for peaceful means—most have little doubt that were Iran to achieve full nuclear capability, its first target would be Israel.

Anyone who follows the news at all continues these days to hear speculation—and it's growing stronger by the month and year—that Israel isn't about to wait for Iran to achieve its nuclear goals. Instead, the likelihood becomes increasingly apparent that Israel may well launch a preemptive attack on Iran to remove that nuclear threat.

As this book goes to press, a new Iranian president is putting on a new face for Iran. Prime Minister Benjamin Netanyahu calls this new face the Iranian "charm offensive." Ron Ben-Yishai calls it an "Iranian honey trap."[1]

> "WASHINGTON—US National Security Adviser Susan Rice attempted to assuage the concerns of Israel and other US-allies in the Middle East over the possibility that Washington would fall for an Iranian ploy to buy time in its pursuit of a nuclear weapon."— Yitzhak Benhorin, published 09.29.13, *Israel News*.[2]

What many don't know is that the same Bible that sets forth the story of Abraham, Isaac, and Ishmael is filled with divine prophecies. Many of those have already come to pass. Some are being fulfilled even at this moment. But the Bible also predicts what is yet to come—including surprising detail concerning the rise and hegemonic goals of a determined Islam.

This book will address in detail some of those Bible prophecies. But in this chapter, we'd like to share at least one possible scenario for what could happen—based on a reasonable projection of what is now coming together in current world events and on what the Bible itself says WILL happen—in the very near future.

Of course, any future scenario includes speculation and perhaps a bit of creative imagination. But this scenario is not random or pulled from thin air—it truly is an educated projection of the Bible's own prophecies (which we'll examine together in the chapters just following this one). The sure word of prophecy only tells us the end result—which this author believes points convincingly to an Islamic Caliphate planted in Jerusalem, along with a third and final Jihad. How we get to this end is anyone's guess. Therefore, what follows is just that—a possible yet reasonable scenario based on considering history, Bible prophecy, and current events.

So how might the stage be set for the restoration of a global caliphate? Could it involve a powerful charismatic Islamic Jihadist stepping into the leadership vacuum left by the Arab Spring uprisings? Jihadists will gladly follow such a person, giving their lives to ensure the establishment of a

---

1.   <http://www.ynetnews.com/articles/0,7340,L-4434217,00.html>.
2.   <http://www.ynetnews.com/articles/0,7340,L-4434492,00.html>.

caliphate. Could it in fact involve Iran achieving nuclear capability—a nation that boasts that when they have nukes, they won't wait a day to use them? Could it be that a sudden attack on Israel by one or more of its Arab neighbors would trigger a series of events leading to the astonishing outcome of a new caliph ruling from headquarters on the mountain ridge of three peaks in Jerusalem known collectively as the Mount of Olives?

Consider one possible scenario (and again, this is only one possibility of many, yet not an unreasonable one, given present-day events):

> *"There is no way to stabilize the Middle East today without defeating the Iranian regime. The Iranian nuclear program must be stopped."*
> —Former Israel Defense Forces Chief of Staff Moshe Ya'alon, January 2008

> *"Like a cancer cell that spreads through the body, this regime [Israel] infects any region. It must be removed from the body."*
> —Mahmoud Ahmadinejad, Then-President of Iran, May 2011

> *"Israel test-fired a missile from a military base on Wednesday, two days after Prime Minister Benjamin Netanyahu warned of the 'direct and heavy threat' posed by Iran's nuclear program."*
> —Reuters, November 2, 2011

As Israeli intelligence concludes that Iran is finally just too close to full nuclear capability, with the likelihood high that Iran would not hesitate to rain down nuclear destruction on Israel's major cities, Tel Aviv decides to take preemptive action.

It launches a single Jericho III missile high over north-central Iran, carrying an electromagnetic pulse (EMP) warhead, and detonates it. EMP causes non-lethal gamma energy to react with the magnetic field, producing a powerful electromagnetic shock wave that destroys electronic devices. *The London Sunday Times* of September 9, 2012, carried a story on just such a possibility, entitled "Israeli gamma pulse 'could send Iran back to Stone Age.'"

There would be no blast—and no radiation effects on the ground. But such a strike could cripple Iran's power grid with electromagnetic pulses, disabling all electronics—especially those integral to the country's nuclear plants. Estimates are that Iran's uranium enrichment centrifuges in Fordo, Natanz, and widely scattered elsewhere, would freeze for decades.

No more computers or cell phones. No more Internet. No more transportation. No more communications systems. No more financial services. Iran would be utterly crippled. The economy would collapse. Chaos would reign. Militarily, Iran would be powerless.

But should we even dream that the rest of the Islamic world—most of it already committed to wiping Israel off the map—would just stand idly by in the wake of such an attack on one of its brother nations? Hardly!

The nightmare that has long filled Washington's politicians with fear and anxiety has arrived. Syria, Egypt, Jordan, Lebanon, even erstwhile U.S. friend Saudi Arabia—all of the major and minor Arab nations—respond with outrage and work furiously and hastily to coordinate their response—the utter annihilation of Israel.

But before World War III can break out...

Back Channels

There's what the media reports.

There's what takes place through formal negotiations and peace talks.

But this is all just the one-eighth of the iceberg visible above the surface.

Hidden below is a world of secrecy and intelligence-gathering and unofficial negotiations—the "back channels" that include so much more than a White House "red phone" or a meeting of ambassadors in some "remote location."

~ ~ ~ ~ ~ ~ ~ ~

At 2:45 a.m., most of the capitol slept. Few would have noticed the steady arrival of limos passing through the White House gate and pulling up to a hidden entrance to the West Wing. Those arriving quickly made their way to the elevators, traveled down, and took their places at the long, lacquered conference table in the basement-level Situation Room.

This was no minor alert. Here in the dead of night, the full National Security Council was assembling. Those present included the President, the Vice President, the Secretaries of Defense and State, the Director of National Intelligence, the National Security Advisor, the Director of the Central Intelligence Agency, the White House Chief of Staff, the Secretary of Homeland Security, and a few other highly placed officials.

"Let's get to it," the President said. Then, to the national intelligence director: "Fill us in."

"Israeli Mossad has learned that Iran has completed their nuclear device and is planning to strike Israel—perhaps within twenty-four hours," began the Director of National Intelligence. Those present understood well that even though Mossad operates in highest secrecy, U.S. intelligence is efficient enough to often discover Israel's most secret plans in advance.

"Our back-channel sources tell us with verifiable certainty that the Defense Minister has just approved and carried out a preemptive EMP strike on Iran that has excised its nuclear sites and totally disabled all its electronically operated systems on the ground. It is now militarily, economically, and in all other respects a completely disabled nation.

"Mr. President, ladies and gentlemen, the surrounding Arab nations are in final preparations to militarily and massively retaliate against Israel, with the goal of its complete destruction. We cannot allow this commencement of hostilities. If they are permitted to occur, it will quickly involve the West on one hand and China and Russia on the other, leading directly to a worldwide conflict and catastrophe."

More brief reports, from State, the CIA, and Defense.

A priority phone rang for the President. "This is the President," he answered. Long moments passed as the President listened.

"I see," he replied. "Are you quite sure this will work? How soon could you communicate with Arab-nation and Israeli leadership? Thank you— I'll present this to our NSC and return your call in minutes—we realize the urgency."

With that, the President ended the call and turned to his council.

"We may have a viable option to get us past this mess," he said. "The call was from the President of Turkey. But his proposal isn't without a downside."

The President then presented to the NSC a summary of the Turkish proposal. The looming response of Israel's neighbors, Turkey rightly noted, would indeed doubtless devolve into a global—and likely all-out—nuclear war.

"So here is what Turkey proposes," the President continued.

To avoid a global nuclear conflict, Turkey was urging that it immediately move to set up in Jerusalem the headquarters of a restored Islamic caliphate, centralizing the efforts and leadership of the entire Islamic world as once existed in the "glory days" of the old Ottoman Empire. But

Turkey also had one more requirement that the NSC knew would create a firestorm of opposition in the United States: Israel must accept its dissolution as a nation, its territory moving under the sovereign control of the Arab-Islamic world.

In exchange, Turkey—with the largest and most powerful military in the Islamic world—would apply all pressure necessary—threats or inducements—to prevent other Arab nations from initiating military action against Israel. For its part, Israel would have little choice but to allow Turkey to immediately set up a restored caliphate in Jerusalem. Either that, or be annihilated.

Given the grim prospect of imminent and virtually certain global war, the Security Council quickly moved to support the Turkish proposal. To put it bluntly, many on the council realized that essentially, they were throwing their long-time ally Israel under the bus. But Israel's own action in attacking Iran had put the U.S. and its allies "over the barrel," so to speak. Faced with the near-certain likelihood of nuclear conflagration or sacrificing Israel and accepting Turkey's price for peace, the council felt it had no choice but to favor the Turkish proposal.

To the Secretaries of State and Defense, the President said: "Get this to Israel immediately through our back channels." Then he reached for the phone—first to reach the President of Turkey. Second, to reach the Prime Minister of Israel. Third, to inform Russia and China.

In the hours and days just ahead, Turkey succeeded in persuading (or sometimes threatening) its fellow Arab-Islamic nations to stand down against Israel. But Turkey lost no time in also carrying through on its intent to set up the caliphate on the ridge of the Mount of Olives in Jerusalem, overlooking the Dome of the Rock and the Al-Aqsa Mosque—the third-holiest site in Islam, after the Masjid al-Haram Mosque in Mecca and the Al-Masjid an-Nabawi Mosque in Medina, both in Saudi Arabia. Temporarily, the caliphate headquarters were located in the BYU Jerusalem Center overlooking the Temple Mount.

The leading role Turkey had played in avoiding a global conflict and restoring the caliphate made it easy for Turkey's President to find the support needed to become the first caliph of Islam since 1924.

What happens next? What may we reasonably see as likely, given current events and the witness of Bible prophecy? Consider this possibility (and again, this continuing scenario is my own projection of what *could* happen, given the direction of current developments in our world):

For a brief time, the new caliph focused on practical matters, but soon enough, he announced the rule of Sharia law throughout all Islamic territories, including now, the recent land of Israel—now known once again as Palestine, an Arab-Islamic territory. Israelis living there could either comply with living under Sharia law—or emigrate to other countries.

Once Islam's new caliph in Jerusalem has completed a new caliphate headquarters somewhere on the ridge of the Mount of Olives and has declared Sharia law binding on all followers of Islam, he issues a call that can only come from a caliph in power. In sinister words that bring immediate alarm to non-Islamic countries, he declares a third and final Islamic Jihad, with the goal of bringing all remaining nations of the world—including the United States and Europe—under the domination of Islam and Sharia law. This Third Jihad corresponds to the "third woe" of Bible prophecy, as set forth in Revelation 11 (more on the three Jihads/three woes in chapters 4 through 6).

Jihadist attacks that make 9/11 seem minor swiftly occur as Islam responds to the caliph's call to Jihad. So-called "dirty bombs" bring death to thousands in such U.S. cities as New York, Los Angeles, Chicago, and Houston—as well as such European capitals as London, Paris, Madrid, and Berlin. Then suicide Jihadists go the next step: carrying suitcase nuclear devices, they detonate their bombs in London and New York. The toll rises to tens of thousands.

The United States, among other nations, has been brought to its knees.

And to its knees, it literally goes. The Pope says that God's judgments are falling on the world for its rejection of Him and His ways. Evangelical leaders in America join members of the U.S. Congress in calling for legislation to get the nation back to God. They are convinced that God is unhappy with this country for a host of reasons—everything from abortion to same-sex marriages to allowing "God's chosen people" to be swept under the bus. They see in the overwhelming calamities on every hand, the judgments of an unhappy God.

Can it be, some wonder, if a sobering meaning might be found in the Jihadic attacks and surging determination of the Islamic world to win the clash of civilizations—to emerge with the entire world under its control? Can it be, perhaps, that God is using Islam as an instrument of His judgmental discipline on those nations that have departed from Him?

The Old Testament of the Bible records many instances in which God used the pagan or heathen or godless nations around His chosen nation of Israel, later also including Judah, to visit His judgments—His discipline—on them.

Catholics, Protestants, charismatic believers, New Agers, even those till now of no faith—all steadily reach the conclusion that something must be done to show God that they mean to return to Him in confession and true repentance. And their most immediate thought is that the best way to demonstrate their return to God is to *start going back to church.*

Growing pressure builds for some kind of legislation to make church attendance the law of the land. After all, this would not be a first, even in the United States. The very first law requiring church attendance on Sunday was enacted in the colony of Virginia in 1610 and read as follows:

> "Every man and woman shall repair in the morning to the divine service and sermons preached upon the Sabbath day, and in the afternoon to divine service, and catechizing, upon pain for the first fault to lose their provision and the allowance for the whole week following; for the second, to lose the said allowance and also be whipt; and for the third to suffer death."[3]

Did you get that? Attend services both morning and afternoon—or face the early-American version of "three strikes and you're out." Strike one: lose your food allowance for a week. Strike two: lose your food allowance for a week and be whipped. Strike three: kiss your life goodbye. And this was not some totalitarian country, some atheistic dictatorship such as China or North Korea or Cuba. Nor was it some theocratic regime such as Iran. This was America.

Other colonies besides Virginia had their own Sunday laws, requiring attendance at services and forbidding everything from working to sports and recreation to swearing and "tippling" at the taverns. Punishments included fines of money and up to 200 pounds of tobacco, being locked in the public stocks, jail time, and again, in "grievous" cases, death.

Captain Kemble of Boston, Massachusetts, was in 1656 locked in the public stocks for two hours for kissing his wife on the Sabbath (Sunday) after spending three years at sea. The charge? "Unseemly behavior."

Even newly elected president George Washington was not exempt from punishment under Sabbath laws. As he traveled from Connecticut

---

3. From "Articles, Lawes, and Orders, Divine, Politique, and Martiall for the Colony of Virginea," in William Strachey, *For the Colony in Virginea Britannia: Lawes, Divine, Morall and Martiall, Etc.* (London: Walter Barre, 1612), 1-7, 19.

to a town in New York to attend worship service one Sunday in 1789, Washington was detained by a tithingman for violating Connecticut's law forbidding unnecessary travel on Sunday. Washington was permitted to continue on his journey only after he promised to go no farther than his destination town.

So given the overwhelming calamities befalling America, it would not be at all surprising if the people of this country called for their legislators to enact a federal Sunday law for the good of families, for the good of the economy, and as a way to turn this nation back to its roots—faith in God. And Congress does not hesitate to pass the necessary laws.

Despite the new legislation, national calamities don't seem to abate, and many conclude that God cannot show His mercy until the nation is united in reverencing Him by keeping Sunday as a day of rest and worship. So new supplemental legislation is passed, mandating that those who fail to come into line will be punished—perhaps by the forfeiture of the right to buy and sell—economic boycott (see Revelation 13:17).

Meanwhile, with the uniting of the Muslim nations under the caliphate, Islam is strengthening its position amongst the nations and the goal of instituting Sharia law throughout the world in response to Allah's command seems attainable. Islam has already slammed the West hard with its bombs. Now it lays plans to do whatever it takes to bring the United States and its allies into submission to the rule of Allah.

The Western world begins to mobilize its still-formidable military forces to keep Islam in check. They realize the stakes. They know full well that this greatest-ever clash of earthly powers will undoubtedly lead to a third great world war—to a biblical Armageddon. But the issue now is survival, and when survival itself is at stake, nations will do whatever it takes to survive.

The West—angered by the horrific devastation wrought by Islam's dirty bomb and nuclear attacks in which millions died and in full survival mode—begins a massive counter-attack, in the early stages of which, the Turkish caliph and caliphate is brought to his end.

Infuriated by the West's strike in removing the caliph, the entire Islamic world unites in rage and, with the backing of Russia and China, mobilizes itself to annihilate the forces of the West. For its part, the West is equally determined to once and for all eliminate the threat of Islam's forces, even if that means emptying its entire nuclear arsenal on them.

The nations on either side of this titanic clash of civilizations marshal their armies for the battle of Armageddon. It looks as if the end of human civilization is about to take place.

But to learn how events ultimately develop—and when—we now need to dig deeper into the prophecies of Daniel, chapter 11. There, we find an accurate preview of tomorrow's headlines.

CHAPTER THREE

PREVIEWING TOMORROW'S HEADLINES

Even based only on what is currently happening in our world, it would not be unreasonable to envision the scenarios and future developments outlined in this book.

Even based on increasing tensions in the always-volatile Middle East— on the growing threat of terrorism—on the clearly stated goals for the future issuing from present-day Islam—even based on these factors alone, one can see that events are rapidly converging toward something ominous, something that will change our world forever.

But we need not rely only on current events to project what may happen in the future. An ancient prophetic voice predicts in precise detail what is just ahead of us. In the Bible's books of Daniel and Revelation, we are able today to preview tomorrow's headlines. In particular, Daniel chapter 11 accurately prophesies what is coming next to this world— what is imminent and certain.

Now, if you are a devout Muslim reading this book, I want to assure you that in the Christian Bible, your role in the near future of this world is prophesied. Your rise to a place of great influence in this world is predicted in that Bible. You are about to play an enormously important role in future events—events that will usher in the final end of this world of pain and misery and death and prepare the way for a new world of eternal peace.

If you are a Christian or of the Jewish faith, you may have heard that the Bible has little or nothing to say about the rise of Islam near the end of our earth's history. Nothing could be farther from the truth. In the chapters just ahead, we will explore in detail what Bible prophecy has to say on this major world development.

If you are a Hindu, Buddhist, atheist, or claim no religious faith at all, you still owe it to yourself to consider what long-ago predictions have to say about what is happening on earth *right now*—and where all the turbulence and instability in this world is leading.

What, after all, do we hear or read about each day in the news? Steep moral decline here in the West as Judeo-Christian principles are steadily abandoned and even mocked. An economic system teetering on the verge of collapse. Ominous global changes in our environment, as the earth groans under the impact of pollution and diminishing resources. Freakish weather and a great increase in natural disasters. Conflict everywhere, it seems—wars all around the globe and a growing threat of terrorism. Longstanding tensions between East and West, between the Judeo-Christian world and Islam, and between Israelis and Arabs. Rampant hunger and starvation in the Third World—and the steady adulteration of the food supply in the First World. Emerging pandemic threats—and in the United States, a healthcare system in utter disarray. And in view of all these urgent and critical problems, paralysis and gridlock among leaders tasked with finding solutions.

Something, many are concluding, has *got* to give! And it does. And it will.

The bad news is that things are going to get worse—unimaginably worse—before they ever get better. The good news is that when things finally do get better as this world reaches its end, a new world beyond will be free of ALL the problems we've just noted. It will be a place of perfect joy and peace beyond all description.

Daniel and the Revelation

With this said, I invite you to come with me back to the mid-1800s. A man who at the age of 12 lost a leg—amputated above the knee—to an infection and later invented an artificial leg with movable joints, is engrossed in studying the ancient prophecies of the Bible books of Daniel and Revelation. As a young man, he became a member of the fledgling Seventh-day Adventist Church and soon became not only an officer of its main headquarters staff but the editor of its leading magazine—*The Advent Review and Sabbath Herald*.

Uriah Smith would in time pull together his own study of Daniel and Revelation, adding in the results of the research of a few of his colleagues, and assemble a book that to this day is one of the most-respected and primary reference works on these two Bible books: *Daniel and the Revelation* (available for sale or free download at: www.*daniel*1145.com). As he delved into the 11th chapter of Daniel, Uriah came across such terms as *the king of the north, the king of the south, glorious holy mountain*—and others. Who were these kings? Where were these places? Smith was, if anything, a careful scholar and researcher. He plunged into history to see how it related to this 11th chapter. And the conclusions he then reached by putting side by side two sources—history and Scripture—led him to confidently identify the people and places of Daniel 11.

There are those who have reached other conclusions about these verses, but Uriah Smith's analysis of them has stood the test of time and remains, in the opinion of this author, the most logical and reasonable explanation of this key Bible passage yet to be presented. It best harmonizes with the record of history and what we see developing in our world today—especially the rise and growing role of Islam.

Daniel 11

So with this background, let's take a moment to look briefly at the key verses of Daniel chapter 11 that indeed, preview tomorrow's headlines, as well as making sense of today's headlines too.

> **"And at the time of the end shall the *king of the south* push at him: and the *king of the north* shall come against him like a whirlwind, with chariots, and with horsemen, and with many ships; and he shall enter into the countries, and shall overflow and pass over."**—Daniel 11:40.

Uriah Smith concluded, based on comparing relevant historical documents to the plain reading of the text, that the "king of the north" in Daniel 11 was the ruler of that territory where modern Turkey now resides, and the "king of the south" in Daniel 11 was the ruler of the territory of Egypt. To reach an understanding of how Smith reached his conclusions, let's take a look at some selected verses—3, 4, and 20:

> **"And a mighty king shall stand up, that shall rule with great dominion, and do according to his will. And when he shall stand up, his kingdom shall be broken, and shall be divided toward the four winds of heaven."**—Daniel 11:3, 4.

A mighty king. A kingdom divided four ways. What does history tell us that could fit these verses? Respected Bible commentaries see the "mighty king" as Alexander the Great. And when he died, his four generals—Cassander, Lysimachus, Ptolemy, and Seleucus—divided his kingdom into four divisions, just as predicted in the verses above. After a few years of infighting, there remained only Seleucus in the north and Ptolemy in the south. Uriah Smith taught that the king of the south referred to whoever the ruler was who occupied the original territory of Ptolemy, located in the southern division of Alexander's kingdom, and that the king of the north referred to whoever the ruler was who occupied the original territory of Lysimachus—which was later taken over by Seleucus—located in the northern division of what was Alexander's kingdom. (See this link[1] for a color version of the map below):

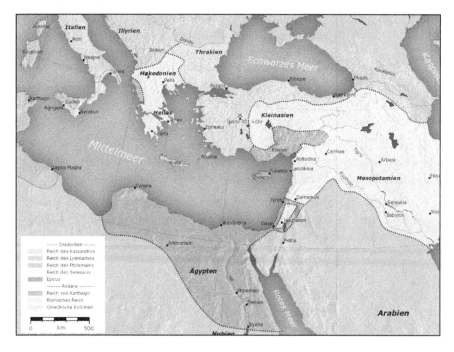

Let's now look at Daniel 11:20:

"Then shall stand up in his estate a raiser of taxes in the glory of the kingdom: but within few days he shall be destroyed, neither in anger, nor in battle."

Who is this "raiser of taxes"?

---

1.   <http://en.wikipedia.org/wiki/Ptolemaic_Kingdom>.

"And it came to pass in those days, that there went out a decree from Caesar Augustus, that all the world should be taxed."—Luke 2:1.

And yes, Caesar Augustus died, not in anger or in battle but peacefully in his bed. No symbolism is found in these verses—just cryptic and straightforward statements. Uriah Smith believed that all the verses in Daniel 11 were just like these three verses—and that very few words in this chapter had been symbolized by the angel Gabriel to mean something different from the plain reading of the text.

Regarding this 11th chapter, Smith writes:

"We now enter upon a prophecy of future events, clothed not in figures and symbols, as in the visions of chapter 2, 7, and 8, but given mostly in plain language. Many of the signal events of the world's history, from the days of Daniel to the end of the world, are here brought to view."—Uriah Smith, *Daniel and the Revelation*, 1912, 247.

The prophecies of chapter 11 are quite unique in how they provide such fine details concerning the interactions of civil powers (see Appendix A, page 103, where the entire 11th chapter is interpreted verse by verse). All of these prophecies would likely have made local news headlines at the time of their fulfillment. It's as if the angel compiled CNN news headlines of the region surrounding the Middle East, from the time of Daniel right up until the close of probation, so that we could catch the steady tread of the events or waymarks ordained by God to take place before the end of the world.

The *close of probation,* by the way, is that time beyond which, the Bible says, the door to salvation is no longer open—each person has made his or her final, irrevocable choice, which God accepts and recognizes:

"He that is unjust, let him be unjust still: and he which is filthy, let him be filthy still: and he that is righteous, let him be righteous still: and he that is holy, let him be holy still. And, behold, I come quickly; and my reward is with Me, to give every man according as his work shall be."—Revelation 22:11, 12.

By comparing current headline news with the prophecies of Daniel 11, we can see where we are in the stream of time. God wants us to know when the end of probation nears so that it does not overtake us as a thief in the night. Daniel 12:1 says: "And at that time shall Michael stand up, the great prince which standeth for the children of thy people." This is when human probation closes—and it's the focal point of this entire prophecy.

Let's look at the last verse of Daniel 11—verse 45 (emphasis supplied):

> **"And *he* shall plant the tabernacles of *his* palace between the seas in the glorious holy mountain; yet *he* shall come to *his* end, and none shall help *him*."**

Let's see if we can decipher what this text is talking about. First, who is this *he, him,* and *his* being referred to here? We have to trace that personal pronoun back to its noun.

This takes us back to verse 40 (emphasis added):

> **"And at the time of the end shall the king of the south push at him: and the *king of the north* shall come against him like a whirlwind, with chariots, and with horsemen, and with many ships; and he shall enter into the countries, and shall overflow and pass over."**

By carefully tracing the pronouns back, we find that they refer to the king of the north (see Appendix B, page 115). This phrase, *king of the north*, is mentioned in chapter 11, verses 6, 7, 8, 11, 13, 15, and 40.

In verses 6 through 15 the king of the north consistently refers to the ruler who controlled the northern portion of Alexander's former kingdom (Asia Minor). History tells us the name of each king of the north mentioned (see Appendix A, page 103). So consistency requires that the king of the north in verse 40 must also be a named person who is ruling this same northern territory.

The phrase *king of the south* is mentioned in chapter 11, verses 5, 9, 11, 14, 25, and 40. As with the king of the north, so likewise, the king of the south consistently refers to a ruler who controlled the southern portion of Alexander's former kingdom—Egypt (see Appendix A, page 103, for the names of each king of the south). An important prophetic hermeneutic (principle of interpretation) is consistency; so again, the king of the south in verse 40 must also be a named person who is ruling this same southern territory.

A careful reading of verse 40 reveals a three-way battle—the king of the south, "him," and the king of the north.

Is there a battle in recent history that involved the ruler of Egypt, the ruler of Asia Minor, and the "him"? (This "him" refers to the king of verses 36-39, which is France—see Appendix C, page 119.)

History records a battle that fits this three-way battle to a T. This battle is known in history as The French Campaign in Egypt and Syria.[2] Notice the perfect fit of Bible prophecy here, with its actual fulfillment in history—in verses 40 through 44. Follow this carefully:

40. And at the time of the end shall the king of the south (*south* still representing Egypt, as identified in Daniel 11:5-15. The leaders of Egypt were Ibrahim Bey and Murad Bey—Egyptian Mameluke rulers—see Appendix D, page 127) **push at him:** (the king of verse 36, which was France, in the person of Napoleon. Egypt pushed against the invasion of France in 1798.) **and the king of the north** (Caliph Selim III of Turkey, the territory of the king of the north— see Daniel 11:5-15) **shall come against him** (France. Turkey declared war on France in 1798) **like a whirlwind, with chariots, and with horsemen, and with many ships;** (Lord Nelson's fleet of ships supported Turkey in its war with France) **and he** (king of the north—Caliph Selim III of Turkey) **shall enter into the countries, and shall overflow and pass over** (the phrase *overflow and pass over* tells us who prevailed in this battle just described. History records that the Turks prevailed, thus we can be certain that the identity of the pronoun *he* in this sentence is the king of the north. This lets us know that the remaining pronouns in this chapter all refer to the king of the north).

41. He (Caliph Selim III of Turkey) **shall enter also into the glorious land** (Palestine)**, and many countries** (*countries* is a supplied word and thus is not in the original Hebrew language in which this chapter in the book of Daniel was written) **shall be overthrown:** (The Turks reclaimed the territory of Palestine which Napoleon had just taken) **but these shall escape out of his** (Caliph Selim III of Turkey) **hand, even Edom and Moab, and the chief children of Ammon** (Edom, Moab, and Ammon, the territory of Jordan, lying outside the limits of Palestine, south and east of the Dead Sea and the Jordan, were out of the line of march of the Turks from Syria to Egypt, so they escaped the ravages of that campaign).

42. He (Caliph Selim III of Turkey) **shall stretch forth his hand also upon the countries: and the land of Egypt shall not escape** (Egypt once more came under the control of the Turks).

43. But he (Caliph Selim III of Turkey) **shall have power over the treasures of gold and of silver, and over the precious things of Egypt:** (Egyptians paid annually to the Turkish government a certain amount of gold and silver, and 600,000 measures of corn,

---

2.   <http://en.wikipedia.org/wiki/French_campaign_in_Egypt_and_Syria>.

and 400,000 of barley) **and the Libyans and the Ethiopians shall be at his steps** (the unconquered Arabs, who sought the friendship of the Turks and were tributary to them at that time).

44. But tidings (intelligence reports) **out of the east** (Persia—today's territory of Iran) **and out of the north** (Russia) **shall trouble him** (Caliph Abdülmecid I of Turkey): **therefore he** (Caliph Abdülmecid I of Turkey) **shall go forth with great fury to destroy, and utterly to make away many** (fulfilled by the Crimean War of 1853-1856, in which Russia and Persia conspired together to destroy the Ottoman Empire but failed in their attempt). For a detailed commentary on these five verses see Appendix E, page 131.

There it is. A more perfect fit of prophecy to history could not be had!

This now brings us up to the final, pivotal verse of the chapter—Daniel 11:45 (emphasis added):

> **"And he *shall plant the tabernacles of his palace* between the seas in the glorious holy mountain; yet he shall come to his end, and none shall help him."**

This word *palace* that the angel Gabriel uses in verse 45 is a foreign word. Nowhere else is it used in the Bible. Why would Gabriel give Daniel a foreign word? And why does he use the word *tabernacles?*

Perhaps something was going to be planted that was not in existence in Daniel's day, so the angel had to use a phrase that would not be understood until the time came for its fulfillment.

An Islamic Caliphate, as we've noted, is a religious/civil system of governance. Is it reasonable to conclude that this unique phrase, *tabernacles* (religious connotation) *of his palace* (civil connotation), could refer to the Islamic Caliphate?

I believe that this phrase could very well be referring to a complex of buildings that will be the headquarters for the world-wide religious/civil ruling caliphate that the king of the north will be planting in the glorious holy mountain.

Let's next look at this phrase *glorious holy mountain* (Daniel 11:45 emphasis added):

> **"And he shall plant the tabernacles of his palace between the seas in the *glorious holy mountain*; yet he shall come to his end, and none shall help him."**

Let's define the words in our phrase:

A *mountain* is defined as "a land mass that projects well above its surroundings." *Holy* is defined as "belonging to, derived from, or associated with a divine power," and *glorious* is "possessing or deserving glory." Glory—"a state of high honor."

Okay, so we are looking for a raised land mass that will be associated with God and which will have a high state of honor.

We are given another clue—we are told that it's going to be located between two seas.

Follow me closely now. I am going to tell you about a spot on Planet Earth that fits this description perfectly. It is the mount where the city of God, New Jerusalem, will someday be located. The apostle John saw in vision the capital city of the universe—"that great city, the holy Jerusalem, descending out of heaven from God" Revelation 21:10.

Yes, according to the book of Revelation, this planet is going to get a makeover and become the home of God and the location of His capital city, New Jerusalem. Listen to what John wrote:

"And I saw a new heaven and a new earth: for the first heaven and the first earth were passed away; and there was no more sea. And I John saw the holy city, new Jerusalem, coming down from God out of heaven, prepared as a bride adorned for her husband. And I heard a great voice out of heaven saying, Behold, the tabernacle of God is with men, and he will dwell with them, and they shall be his people, and God himself shall be with them, and be their God. And God shall wipe away all tears from their eyes; and there shall be no more death, neither sorrow, nor crying, neither shall there be any more pain: for the former things are passed away. And he that sat upon the throne said, Behold, I make all things new. And he said unto me, Write: for these words are true and faithful." — Revelation 21:1-5.

The capital city of the universe has a spot of real estate already picked out for it. Listen to what the ancient prophet Zechariah wrote:

"And his feet shall stand in that day upon the mount of Olives, which is before Jerusalem on the east, and the mount of Olives shall cleave in the midst thereof toward the east and toward the west, and there shall be a very great valley; and half of the mountain shall remove toward the north, and half of it toward the south. . . . And it shall be in that day, that living waters shall go out from Jerusalem; half of them toward the former sea, and

half of them toward the hinder sea: in summer and in winter shall it be."— Zechariah 14:4, 8.

That's right, the Mount of Olives—that raised land mass that overlooks the current city of Old Jerusalem, the very spot from which Jesus ascended when He returned to heaven 2,000 years ago, a location that is currently between two seas (Dead Sea and the Mediterranean Sea) and in the earth made new will still be between two seas, according to Zechariah—on this glorious holy mountain will reside New Jerusalem, the city of God.

One more piece of evidence for locating the glorious holy mountain: Jesus told His followers that the city of Jerusalem would be destroyed:

"And Jesus went out, and departed from the temple: and his disciples came to him for to show him the buildings of the temple. And Jesus said unto them, See ye not all these things? verily I say unto you, There shall not be left here one stone upon another, that shall not be thrown down."— Matthew 24:1, 2.

Jesus gave them a sign to look for so they could "get out of Dodge" before it was too late. Here it is, in Matthew 24:15, 16 (emphasis added):

"When ye therefore shall see the abomination of desolation, spoken of by Daniel the prophet, stand in *the holy place*, (whoso readeth, let him understand:) Then let them which be in Judaea flee into the mountains."

The warning sign that they were to look for was seen by the residents of Jerusalem in A.D. 66, when the idolatrous standard of the Roman army, under the command of Cestius, was set up or was seen standing upon the ridge (Mount of Olives) overlooking Jerusalem. The Mount of Olives was considered part of the sacred land that surrounded the city of Jerusalem, so when the Christians saw this sign, they knew that it was time to flee. But how could they flee when they were under siege, completely surrounded by the Romans? Here is what happened:

- ▸ November 14–16, A.D. 66: Cestius attacks and pursues the rebels to Jerusalem. He pitches camp on Mount Scopus (Mount of Olives) for three days to collect food from local villages.

- ▸ November 22, A.D. 66: Cestius suddenly gives up and retreats from the city "without any reason in the world."[3]

When Cestius retreated, the Christians fled the city. Four years later, Jerusalem was destroyed by Titus.

---

3.   <http://www.josephus.org/warChronology2.htm>.

"The closeness of the Mount of Olives to Jerusalem's walls made this series of hills a grave strategic danger. The Roman commander Titus had his headquarters on the northern extension of the ridge during the siege of Jerusalem in A.D. 70. He named the place Mount Scopus, or 'Lookout Hill,' because of the view which it offered over the city walls. The whole hill must have provided a platform for the Roman catapults that hurled heavy objects over the Jewish fortifications of the City."[4]

Titus also pitched his camp on the Mount of Olives in A.D. 70. But this time there was no retreat. The city and temple were destroyed. Not one stone was left upon the other.

The point of all this is that Jesus called the spot where Cestius set up the Roman standard a holy spot—and for good reason. He knew that this would be the very spot where God's throne would one day be located. Jesus steps onto the Mount of Olives at the end of the 1,000 years (see Revelation 20), and from this center spot, a plain spreads out east, west, north, and south and becomes the foundation for the New Jerusalem.

When you think of what this piece of real estate will contain for all eternity—the throne room of Almighty God, the capital of the universe, New Jerusalem—is it any wonder that the angel Gabriel would refer to the Mount of Olives as "the glorious holy mountain"?

Could it be that the leader of Turkey will plant an Islamic Caliphate headquarters on the Mount of Olives, which, as has been mentioned, is located between the two seas—the Mediterranean Sea and the Dead Sea?

The Temple Mount is already crowded with Muslim holy sites. The Mount of Olives overlooks the city and would be a most likely spot for a caliphate headquarters complex.

So here it is—verse 45, the only verse of chapter 11 that has not found a fulfillment in the historical records. Here is a reasonable interpretation of what is yet to transpire, based upon a literal reading of the text and using the same interpretive approach that has so clearly revealed the historical fulfillment of the previous 44 verses:

And he (the king of the north—the leader of Turkey) **shall plant** (place or establish) **the tabernacles of his palace** (a religious/political entity—Islamic Caliphate) **between the seas** (Mediterranean and Dead Seas) **in the glorious holy mountain** (Mount of Olives); **yet he** (the king of the north) **shall come to his end, and none shall**

---

4.   <http://www.bible-history.com/jesus/jesusuntitled00000453.htm>.

help him (something will happen that brings the rule of the king of the north to an end).

Verse 45 is the last waymark of Daniel 11, and after this waymark is fulfilled, Daniel 12:1 will take place:

"And at that time shall Michael stand up, the great prince which standeth for the children of thy people: and there shall be a time of trouble, such as never was since there was a nation [even] to that same time: and at that time thy people shall be delivered, every one that shall be found written in the book."

This time of trouble will include the battle of Armageddon—a titanic clash of civilizations. But before that takes place, the third of the three great "Woes" of Revelation 9 and 11 will first strike the West. Those woes correspond perfectly to the Three Jihads of Islam—two in past history and one yet to come. We now turn from Daniel to Revelation, to explore what the Bible has to say about those three Woes/Jihads.

CHAPTER FOUR

THE FIRST WOE - THE FIRST JIHAD

Woe is me!

Likely, you've heard others say that many times in your life. Likely, you've even said it yourself.

A phrase once used by Isaiah the prophet (Isaiah 6:5), its awareness grew when Shakespeare employed it in *Hamlet*, Act 3, Scene 1. But the phrase has been challenged by a former editor at *The New York Times Book Review*, Patricia T. O'Conner, whose best-selling grammar guide, *Woe Is I*, makes the case that *her* book title is the more correct way to state the words.

But between Isaiah's use of the phrase and Shakespeare's, the prophet John wrote in Revelation—the Bible's last book—these words:

"And I beheld, and heard an angel flying through the midst of heaven, saying with a loud voice, Woe, woe, woe, to the inhabiters of the earth."—Revelation 8:13.

Woe? How about *Triple Woe?* And woe is not just to me—but to all "inhabiters of the earth."

In this and the next two chapters, we're going to examine these three biblical woes of Revelation and notice the clear parallels they have with the three great Jihads of Islam—the first two, part of past history, and the third, yet future.

Buckle up, then, because this chapter isn't going to be lightweight fluff,

I promise you that. We're going to burrow deeply into both Bible prophecy and history. Take it slow if you need to—stop now and then and even back up and re-read a paragraph or two to be sure you understood each fact and verse, since what follows will build on what's already been covered. It would actually be a real advantage if you had a Bible at hand to which you could refer, as you work your way through this chapter.

The "Sevens" of Revelation

Now, if you study the book of Revelation much, you soon note that it is filled with "sevens"—among them, churches, stars, seals, angels, trumpets, thunders, plagues, and a number of others. Seven is a biblical number connoting perfection or completeness.

Notice how Revelation, chapter 8 begins:

> **"And when he had opened the *seventh seal*, there was silence in heaven about the space of half an hour. And I saw the *seven angels* which stood before God; and to them were given *seven trumpets*."**—Revelation 8:1, 2, emphasis supplied.

Seven seals.

Seven angels.

Seven trumpets.

Let's focus in on the seven angels (or messengers) and their seven trumpets.

In Revelation 8:7-12 we read of the sounding of the first four trumpets. According to many students of history and prophecy, these had to do with the fall of Western Rome brought about by the attacks of the Visigoths, Vandals, Huns, and Heruli in the fifth century.

Then, in the last verse of chapter 8, the final three trumpets sound—each one focused on one of the three "woes," as we noted earlier:

> **"And I beheld, and heard an angel flying through the midst of heaven, saying with a loud voice, Woe, woe, woe, to the inhabiters of the earth by reason of the other voices of the trumpet of the three angels, which are yet to sound!"**—Revelation 8:13.

So trumpets five, six, and seven contain the three woes. We are going to look at these three woes in detail, and in doing this, we will discover something incredible that is taking place right before our eyes—now, in our time—that is setting the stage for Planet Earth's final conflict that the Bible calls Armageddon. We will discover that something is even now in the process of taking place that will be the flashpoint for the battle of Armageddon.

The Battle of Armageddon and the Close of Probation

Armageddon will be a battle fought after the close of probation. When is this close of probation—and what is it?

> **"And at that time shall Michael stand up, the great prince which standeth for the children of thy people: and there shall be a time of trouble, such as never was since there was a nation even to that same time."**—Daniel 12:1.

Michael is one of the Bible's names for Jesus (see Appendix F, page 139). And in this verse, He stands up, in heaven, because He has finished His work there of applying the benefits of His sacrifice on the Cross to every person who has ever lived—to all who have chosen Him to be their Savior from sin. And when He stands up, He closes the door to salvation. He doesn't do this to keep anyone from being saved—He is simply recognizing that all have already made their final decision to accept or reject His salvation. That is why He says, as He "stands up":

> **"He that is unjust, let him be unjust still: and he which is filthy, let him be filthy still: and he that is righteous, let him be righteous still: and he that is holy, let him be holy still."**—Revelation 22:11.

Notice that Daniel 12:1 above says that "at that time," Michael stands up. At *what* time? The answer to that is found in the sentence immediately preceding this verse—Daniel 11:45. In the earlier chapters of the book you're reading, we've already found what happens there:

> **"And he shall plant the tabernacles of his palace between the seas in the glorious holy mountain; yet he shall come to his end, and none shall help him."**—Daniel 11:45.

Remember? To review: "He" (meaning the king of the north—the leader of Turkey) would "plant the tabernacles of his palace" (the headquarters of a restored Islamic caliphate) "between the seas" (the Mediterranean and Dead Seas) "in the glorious holy mountain" (the Mount of Olives in Jerusalem) "yet he" (king of the north) "shall come to his end, and none shall help him" (something will happen that brings the rule of the king of the north to an end).

And THEN, says the very next verse (Daniel 12:1), "shall Michael stand up"—and human probation, its door of salvation, is forever closed.

51

The Battle of Armageddon is to be fought *after* the close of probation. Jumping ahead briefly to verses we'll explore in more detail later, we find that Armageddon will also be fought *at the time of* the sixth plague (Revelation 16:12-14)—and *after* the four angels of heaven have released their hold on the "winds of strife" so those winds are free to work their destruction on the nations of the earth (Revelation 7:1).

When we understand the third woe of the seventh trumpet in direct connection with Daniel 11:45, we will clearly see—by the events taking place right now in the Middle East—that conditions are ripe for the third Jihad/woe to strike. The fact that the third Jihad (which will be the flash point for the battle of Armageddon) is now on the horizon is actually good news. Why? Because the end of this world, with the Second Coming of Jesus, takes place at the time of this battle.

But this message is good news only for those who are prepared spiritually and practically for what is about to happen here on earth—it is *not* good news for those who have not made preparations for this coming crisis (see chapter 7—"Are You Prepared?").

Before we focus in detail on these three woes, remember who is speaking to us:

"The Revelation of Jesus Christ, which God gave unto him, to show unto his servants *things which must shortly come to pass*; and he sent and signified it by his angel unto his servant John: Who bare record of the word of God, and of the testimony of Jesus Christ, and of all things that he saw."—Revelation 1:1, 2, emphasis supplied.

The three woes are messages dictated directly from the heart of God. He wants us to understand the signs of the times and what they mean in relation to His Son's promised return.

As a result of understanding these three woes, our spiritual eyes will be opened to see the prophetic significance of the current War on Terror and the current turmoil in the Middle East. But we won't be able to see any of this unless we know what the *third woe* is. And only by understanding the *first and the second woe* is it possible to know what the third woe will be. So let's get started and take a look at this first woe found in the fifth trumpet:

The First Woe

"And the fifth angel sounded, and I saw a star [fallen] from heaven unto the earth: and to him was given the key of the bottomless pit."—Revelation 9:1.

This first woe begins by noting a fallen star that had come from heaven and was now upon this earth. Angels are sometimes referred to as stars (Revelation 1:20). This star could very well be referring to the fallen angel we call Satan.[1]

"And he opened the bottomless pit; and there arose a smoke out of the pit, as the smoke of a great furnace; and the sun and the air were darkened by reason of the smoke of the pit."—Revelation 9:2.

The fallen star was given the key to the abyss. What does the key represent? It represents power or authority—the ability to unlock, to free, or to release. And what does Revelation 9:2 say he releases? He releases smoke that darkens the sun and air. The sun, of course, represents Christ, the light of the world and the "Sun of righteousness" (Malachi 4:2). It also represents truth. Under this trumpet Satan is permitted to release from his arsenal, falsehood and error that would darken the light of the gospel—that would obscure Jesus, the divine Son of God, the Light of the world, the crucified Saviour of mankind.

What is this *bottomless pit,* or "abyss," as it says in the original Greek language? This term is used seven times in the book of Revelation (Revelation 9:1, 2, 11; 11:7; 17:8; 20:1, 3). In most places where it is used, it represents the domain of Satan. So any power or teaching emerging from the abyss is inspired by him.

The very next verse says that out of the smoke came powerful locusts:

"And there came out of the smoke locusts upon the earth: and unto them was given power, as the scorpions of the earth have power."—Revelation 9:3.

The Bible employs the locust as a symbol of the Arab nations. Speaking of the Midianite Arabs, the Bible says:

"They came as grasshoppers [or locusts] **for multitude."**—Judges 6:5. The original word is *locusts.*

"And the Midianites and the Amalekites [Arab tribes] **. . . lay along the valley like grasshoppers** [locusts] **for multitude."**—Judges 7:12.

---

1. "How art thou fallen from heaven, O Lucifer, son of the morning! how art thou cut down to the ground, which didst weaken the nations!"—Isaiah 14:12.

The Rise of Islam

Question: After the fall of Western Rome in A.D. 476—that is, after the first four trumpets—did a religious movement, arise in Arabia who would obscure the light of the gospel?

The answer is Yes! Only one event fulfills this—and it does so to the very letter. That event was the rise of the Islamic religion in the seventh century A.D.

In the Quran, Islam teaches, for example, that Christ was not the Son of God:

"Creator of the heavens and the earth. How should He have a son when He had no consort? He created all things, and He has knowledge of all things."—Surrah 6:101.

"Allah forbid that He should have a son!"—Surrah 4:171.

Let's move to our next verse in Revelation 9:

"And it was commanded them that they should not hurt the grass of the earth, neither any green thing, neither any tree; but only those men which have not the seal of God in their foreheads."—Revelation 9:4.

Was such a command issued to the Islamic Arab conquerors? Notice that in earlier trumpets—the first trumpet, for example . . .

". . . a third part of trees was burnt up and all green grass was burnt up."—Revelation 8:7.

The Visigoths, who fulfilled the first trumpet, deliberately destroyed the vegetation in Western Europe—so much so that it resulted in the formation of desert areas.

Now, the prediction says that "it was commanded them . . . not to hurt the grass." Was there such a command? The command was issued at the very time when the Islamic Arabs were about to invade the Roman Empire back in the seventh century. They had just raided Persia, and now they were about to invade Syria, the Eastern portion of Eastern Rome. Muhammad had died, and Abu Bakr, his successor, was now in charge.

Here now is the actual command of Revelation 9:4—as recorded in history—that the multitude of locusts were not to hurt the grass or the trees:

"As soon as their numbers were complete, Abubeker ascended the hill, reviewed the men, the horses, and the arms, and poured forth a fervent prayer for the success of their undertaking . . . . 'Remember', said the successor of the prophet, 'that you are always in the presence of God, on the verge of death, in the assurance of judgment, and the hope of paradise. Avoid injustice and oppression; consult with your brethren, and study to preserve the love and confidence of your troops. When you fight the battles of the lord, acquit yourselves like men, without turning your backs; but let not your victory be stained with the blood of women or children. Destroy no palm trees, nor burn any field of corn. Cut down no fruit trees, nor do any mischief to cattle, only such as you kill to eat. When you make a covenant . . . stand to it and be as good as your word. As you go on, you will find some religious persons, who live retired in monasteries, and propose to themselves to serve God that way: let them alone and neither kill them nor destroy their monasteries. And you will find another sort of people that belong to the synagogue of Satan, who have shaven crowns; be sure you cleave their skulls, and give them no quarter, till they either turn Mahometans or pay tribute."[2]

The Islamic Arabs did not destroy any green thing or trees, just as the prophecy of Revelation 9:4 had declared 600 years before. Amazing evidence that "all Scripture is inspired of God."—2 Timothy 3:16.

Now, the prophecy also included the hurting of "those men which have not the seal of God in their foreheads." As seen in the command recorded above by Gibbons, they were to kill the men who had shaven crowns. These were the priests of the Roman Catholic Church. The shaven ring on their crowns represented the sun, which they honored by the day they chose to honor—Sunday—which they incorporated from the sun worship of ancient Babylon.

But is it also correct that those who had "the seal of God" were protected by the Muslim invaders?

What do we understand by the term *the seal of God?* In Revelation 7 the seal of God is shown as being implanted in the foreheads of God's people in the last days, in order to protect them from the judgments of God. Many Bible expositors believe that the seal of God refers to the Sabbath of the fourth commandment (a seal must have three specific elements: the name, the title of authority, and the territory of His dominion). In the fourth commandment we find:

The name: "Lord thy God"

---

2.   Edward Gibbon, *Decline and Fall of the Roman Empire,* vol. V, 489, 490.

The title of authority: Creator—"the Lord made"

The territory of His dominion: "heaven and earth, the sea and all that in them is"

> **"Remember the sabbath day, to keep it holy. Six days shalt thou labour, and do all thy work: But the seventh day is the sabbath of [1]** *the LORD thy God:* **in it thou shalt not do any work, thou, nor thy son, nor thy daughter, thy manservant, nor thy maidservant, nor thy cattle, nor thy stranger that is within thy gates: For in six days [2]** *the LORD made* **[3]** *heaven and earth, the sea, and all that in them is,* **and rested the seventh day: wherefore the LORD blessed the sabbath day, and hallowed it."**—Exodus 20:8-11, emphasis supplied.

So—did the Arabs or Saracens protect those who were observers of the seventh-day Sabbath of the fourth commandment, back there in the seventh century? Notice the record as given by Dr. B. G. Wilkinson in his study of the rise and spread of the early Christian faith.

> "In the early centuries of the Christian era, the church of the East [not the Western or Latin church] sometimes called the Assyrian church, sometimes the Nestorian church [who were observers of the true Sabbath] very effectively spread throughout Asia and the East, but remained separate from the church in the West, especially the apostasy. These true Christians became the teachers of the Saracens and were responsible for establishing an educational system in Syria, Mesopotamia, Turkestan, Tibet, China, India, Ceylon, and other areas."[3]

History has it, then, that the Arabs, like the Persians, were very partial to the Assyrian Christians, because they found it necessary in the early days of their power to make use of the superb schools which the church had developed.

Edward Gibbon confirms Dr. Wilkinson's statement:

> "To his Christian subjects [i.e., the true Christians, not the apostate ones whom the Arabs tormented]; Mohomet readily granted the security of their persons, the freedom of their trade, the property of their goods, and the toleration of their worship."[4]

We move on now to verse 5:

---

3.   B. G. Wilkinson, *Truth Triumphant* (Mountain View, CA: Pacific Press, 1944), 268-291.

4.   Gibbon, *Decline and Fall*, vol. V: 439-W; 579, 580; 390, 391.

"And to them it was given that they should not kill them, but that they should be tormented five months: and their torment was as the torment of a scorpion, when he striketh a man."—Revelation 9:5.

The First Jihad—History's Fulfillment of the Prophesied First Woe

The Muslims were not to kill, but they *were* to hurt and torment. Does this mean that they did not kill in their conquests? No! It could not mean that. The killing concerned the political killing or destroying of the Roman Empire—Eastern Rome. In their battles the Muslims killed hundreds of thousands of people, and they themselves lost hundreds of thousands. During this first great Islamic Jihad—which history says took place between A.D. 622 and 750[5]—they began with conquering Arabia, then later overran almost all of Eastern Rome. They conquered North Africa, then crossed the Straits of Gibraltar and conquered most of Spain and even overran some of Southwestern France. But in all their conquests, they were not able to destroy or kill, or end, the Empire of Eastern Rome. They made concerted efforts to capture Constantinople, the capital of the Empire, but always, they were unsuccessful.

Amid the rampant apostasy in the Roman Empire were remnants of God's faithful people, who were withdrawing to the wilderness regions in order to escape persecution and maintain their faith. These included the Albigenses of South France, the Waldenses of Northern Italy, and others in Bohemia, Germany, and other places. When the Muslims invaded France, they were nearing areas where God's true people were dwelling, and it is believed that one reason the Muslims were repelled was so the people of God would be protected. Moreover, while Catholic Europe was fighting off the Muslims, they were preoccupied with those battles and couldn't pursue God's people.

What does the scorpion's tail in verse 5 (and verse 10) represent? The key is found in the writings of Isaiah in the Old Testament:

"The ancient and honorable, he is the head; and the prophet that teaches lies, he is the tail."—Isaiah 9:15.

The false prophet, the lying prophet—false religion—that is the tail. In other words, the religion of the prophet Muhammad is the tail which tormented men by obscuring the gospel of the only begotten, divine Son of God.

Yes, the one and only Father God, the great Creator God, has always had a Son, according to the Old Testament:

---

5.   <http://www.jihadwatch.org/islam-101.html>.

"Who hath ascended up into heaven, or descended? who hath gathered the wind in his fists? who hath bound the waters in a garment? who hath established all the ends of the earth? what is his name, *and what is his son's name,* if thou canst tell?" —Proverbs 30:4, emphasis supplied.

"For God so loved the world, that he gave *his only begotten Son,* that whosoever believeth in him should not perish, but have everlasting life."—John 3:16, emphasis supplied.

A Prophecy of 150 Days

The prophecy said "that they should be tormented five months." In a prophetic month are exactly thirty days. Therefore, five months would equal 150 days. In symbolic prophecy, a day equals a year;[6] therefore, the 150 days represent 150 years. Notice what the prophecy says would take place during this 150-year period:

▸ The seventh-century opening of the bottomless pit, from which Islam arose through Mohammad.

▸ The seventh-century command to not burn trees and to hurt only those men which have not the seal of God in their foreheads.

So what century should we look at to find the fulfillment of this 150-year prophecy? The seventh century, of course!

To find when this 150-year period of torment by the Muslims began, we need to find the exact year in which the teachings of Mohammad arose from the bottomless pit.

"The Prophet Muhammad . . . proclaimed his prophetic mission in Arabia in 612 and eventually won over the city of his birth, Mecca, to the new faith."[7]

This period of Muslim torment continued until there was a sharp division in the leadership of the Muslim world. As a result, two Islamic caliphates were formed. This occurred in A.D. 756. The new caliph, reigning in Damascus, Syria, transferred his capital to the West Bank of the Tigris and founded the city of Baghdad, where he became the leading caliph of the Muslim Empire. He built his city on a canal flowing from the Euphrates to the Tigris—an area outside the boundaries of the Roman Empire. In A.D. 762 the caliph transferred his capital outside the realm

---

6. <http://en.wikipedia.org/wiki/Day-year_principle>.

7. Helen Chapin Metz, ed. *Iran: A Country Study* (Washington, D.C.: GPO, for the Library of Congress, 1987), chapter: "Islamic Conquest."

of the Roman Empire. With this transfer came a complete change of attitude on the part of the Muslims.

As one church historian wrote:

"The [Arab] conquerors now settled tranquilly in the countries they had subdued."[8]

"From the 8th to the 12th centuries the Muslim world enjoyed great prosperity. Muslim traders were in close contact with three continents and could move goods back and forth between China and Western Europe and from Russia to Central Africa."[9]

The period of conquest and torment had ceased—and it ceased in A.D. 762 A.D. If we deduct 612 from 762, we have *exactly* 150 years or five prophetic months! Thus, this prophetic period in which the Muslims were to torment or hurt men was fulfilled to the very letter—to the very year.

The first Bible scholar to see this 150-year prophecy was an Italian named Joachim of Floris. He saw this in A.D. 1190. On pages 24 and 25 of this footnote,[10] you will find listed 128 others from the twelfth century through the twentieth century who also understood this. A high percentage of them use the date range of A.D. 612-762. You can see from the following map the territory that this first-woe caliphate conquered during this 150-year period.

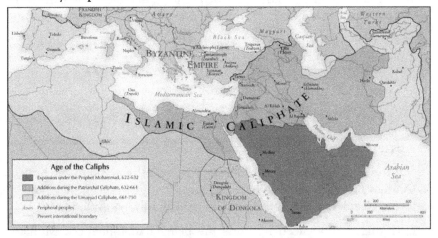

8. George Waddington, *History of the Church, From the Earliest Ages to the Reformation* (London, England: Baldwin, 1833), vol. 2, 44.

9. <http://emayzine.com/index.php/history-103/history-103-week-3/123-the-byzantine-empire-and-islam>.

10. <http://docs.adventistarchives.org/docs/MIN/MIN19440601-V17-06__B.pdf#view=fit>.

In the first ten years of Omar's reign (he was the second successor of Muhammad), Gibbon says:

"The Saracens reduced 36,000 cities or castles, destroyed 4,000 churches and built 1,400 mosques."[11]

Now, other Bible students in the list of 128 in footnote 10 saw the five-month prophecy coming at the *end* of the fifth trumpet period, rather than at the beginning. As I have looked at the reasoning of both views, I have concluded that they are both right. Because of the duplication of symbols in this prophecy, I see *two* five-month periods brought to view. Let me list those symbols that are duplicated:

▶ Bottomless pit (9:1; 9:11)

▶ Leader (9:1—fallen star; 9:11—angel of the bottomless pit)

▶ Scorpion sting (9:5; 9:10)

▶ Five months (9:5; 9:10)

One noticeable feature about apocalyptic prophecy is this: Information is usually given in the least possible amount of words. For this prophecy to mention twice that there will be five months isn't because the apostle John is just being repetitive and wordy. No, such repetition never occurs without good cause. So why are these four things repeated in this fifth trumpet? Simply this: It is because we are to understand that this trumpet *starts* with a five-month period, and it *ends* with a five-month period.

The people of the first period were Arabs—and the people of the second period were Turks. Both groups would be Muslims led by leaders influenced by Satan, the fallen star—the angel of the bottomless pit, using the scorpion sting of falsehood, with a different leader beginning each five-month period. Muhammad was the first leader of the first period. Who was the first leader of the second prophetic time period?

This leader is brought to view in Revelation 9:11:

"And they had a king over them, which is the angel of the bottomless pit, whose name in the Hebrew tongue is Abaddon, but in the Greek tongue hath his name Apollyon."—Revelation 9:11.

This king is influenced by the same being that influenced Muhammad—the fallen star or angel of the bottomless pit. He begins once again the conquest of territory. This king, whose Greek name was Apollyon, was Osman—the founder of the Ottoman Empire. He reigned from 1299-1324.

---

11. Gibbon, *Decline and Fall,* vol. V, 474, 475.

"Ottoman historians often dwell on the prophetic significance of his name, which means 'bone-breaker', signifying the powerful energy with which he and his followers appeared to show in the following centuries of conquest. The name Osman is the Turkish variation of the Muslim name Othman . . ."[12]

Gibbon adds:

"It was on the twenty-seventh of July, in the year 1299, that Othman first invaded the territory of Nicomedia," [in Asia Minor] "and the singular accuracy of the date, seems to disclose some foresight of the rapid and destructive growth of the monster."[13]

This, then, would be the date for the beginning of the *second* 150-year period. From July 27, 1299 to July 27, 1449, the Turks were engaged in almost constant warfare with the Greek Empire, yet without conquering it—just as the prophecy foretold. This beginning date, July 27, 1299, is of vital importance to the second woe (which will be the focus of the next chapter).

Back now to our locusts:

"And the shapes of the locusts were like unto horses prepared unto battle; and on their heads were as it were crowns like gold, and their faces were as the faces of men. And they had hair as the hair of women, and their teeth were as the teeth of lions. And they had breastplates, as it were breastplates of iron; and the sound of their wings was as the sound of chariots of many horses running to battle."—Revelation 9:7-9.

The Muslim warriors are likened to "horses prepared for battle." This also is a true picture of the type of military force that was used by the Muslims in their method of attack.

"I shall here observe what I must often repeat, that the charge of the Arabs was not like that of the Greeks and Romans, the effort of a firm and compact infantry: their military force was chiefly formed of cavalry and archers."[14]

They wore turbans, beards, long hair, and breastplates, just as the prophecy said they would.

"One woe is past; and, behold, there come two woes more hereafter."—Revelation 9:12.

---

12.   <http://en.wikipedia.org/wiki/Osman_I>.

13.   Gibbon, *Decline and Fall*, chap. 64, par. 14.

14.   Ibid., vol. V, 478, 479.

James White, (1821–1881) was ordained a minister of the Christian Connection in 1843. In 1863, he printed a chart that summarized the key prophecies based on the visions of the Bible prophets Daniel and John.

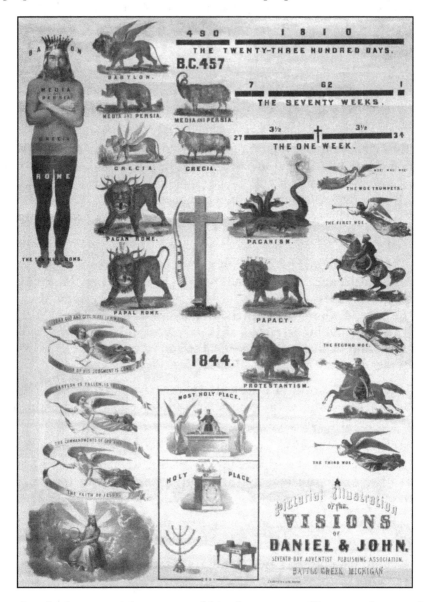

On the bottom right corner of his chart, you will notice the angels blowing the last three woe trumpets. The first woe trumpet is represented by a Muslim with a spear. The second woe trumpet is represented by a Muslim with a musket. The third woe trumpet, being yet future, White couldn't identify and didn't.

One biblical woe—and one corresponding historical Jihad (the Muslim with the spear)—is past. Two more remain. We now turn our attention to the second woe and Jihad (the Muslim with the musket).

CHAPTER FIVE

THE SECOND WOE - THE SECOND JIHAD

*W*oe isn't a word used very widely these days. So since we're now beginning the second of three chapters focusing on the three woes of Revelation 8, let's take a moment to define the word:

▶ "A condition of deep suffering from misfortune, affliction, or grief . . . ruinous trouble"—*Merriam-Webster.*

▶ "Deep distress or misery, as from grief; wretchedness . . . misfortune; calamity."—*American Heritage Dictionary.*

▶ "Grievous distress, affliction, or trouble."—Dictionary.com.

Get the drift? *Woe* is a most unhappy word—a condition or state of utter misery and trouble.

Does this describe what history says about the two Islamic Jihads that have taken place already? I don't think it is possible to calculate the number of lives lost over those several hundred years of Islamic conquest, but no doubt millions of people on both sides lost their lives—the book of Revelation most certainly had it right in predicting these two Jihads as "woes."

We found in the previous chapter that the first great wave of Islamic Jihad took place between A.D. 622 and 750, during which Islam conquered not only its home base of Arabia but expanded to conquer also nearly all of the Eastern Roman Empire. They conquered North Africa, then crossed over into Europe and conquered most of Spain and were finally stopped after subduing some of Southwestern France.

JERUSALEM CALIPHATE AND THE THIRD JIHAD

A Second Jihad

But the drive to conquer did not rest long and rose up again about three centuries later in a second great Jihad, between A.D. 1071 and 1683.[1] Whereas the first Jihad was carried out by Islamic Arabs, this second Jihad was aggression from Islamic Turks. It resulted in the capture of Constantinople (Istanbul), and as it spread, pushed Islamic control deeper into North Africa, farther north into the Balkans, and east into India.

We've discovered that the first woe took place as the fifth angel sounded his trumpet in the first twelve verses of Revelation 9. And that predicted first woe would be fulfilled with precision by the first great Islamic Jihad.

But now, moving on to verse 13, we hear the sixth angel sounding his trumpet:

"And the sixth angel sounded, and I heard a voice from the four horns of the golden altar which is before God, Saying to the sixth angel which had the trumpet, Loose the four angels[2] which are bound in the great river Euphrates."—Revelation 9:13, 14.

Identifying the Second-Woe Power

In the verses that follow, we note several items that nail down the identity of this second-woe power:

"And the four angels were loosed, which were prepared for an hour, and a day, and a month, and a year, for to slay the third part of men. And the number of the army of the horsemen were two hundred thousand thousand: and I heard the number of them. And thus I saw the horses in the vision, and them that sat on them, having breastplates of fire, and of jacinth, and brimstone: and the heads of the horses were as the heads of lions; and out of their mouths issued fire and smoke and brimstone. By these three was the third part of men killed, by the fire, and by the smoke, and by the brimstone, which issued out of their mouths. For their power is in their mouth, and in their tails:

---

1. <http://www.jihadwatch.org/islam-101.html>.
2. The Four Angels: These were the four principal sultans of which the Ottoman Empire was composed, located in the country watered by the great river Euphrates. These sultans were situated at Aleppo, Iconium, Damascus, and Bagdad. Previously they had been restrained; but God commanded, and they were loosed.—Uriah Smith, *Daniel and the Revelation* (1897), 508.

for their tails were like unto serpents, and had heads, and with them they do hurt."—Revelation 9:15-19.

In these verses we see an army of 200 "thousand thousand"[3] horsemen poised to invade the "third part" of the Roman Empire. What is this *third part* we keep hearing about in the trumpets? In the first four trumpets were twelve mentions of this phrase, "the third part." For example, the third part of:

▶ The trees—Revelation 8:7.

▶ The sea—Revelation 8:8.

▶ The ships—Revelation 8:9.

▶ The rivers—Revelation 8:10.

▶ The sun, moon, and stars—Revelation 8:12.

When the Bible speaks of one third, this is not necessarily an exact mathematical proportion. It is simply an expression to denote that the punishment of God is not total destruction (see Zechariah 13:8, 9; Ezekiel 5:1-4, 12).

During the first four trumpets the western portion of the Roman Empire was destroyed. Under the fifth trumpet (the first woe) the Eastern Roman Empire was not destroyed—only tormented. And under this sixth trumpet (the second woe) this Eastern part of the Roman Empire is finally destroyed.

Who were these horsemen that destroyed this part of the Empire? After the battles of the fifth-trumpet Islamic caliphate, what power invaded Eastern Rome and destroyed it? History tells us that it was the Islamic Turkomans, or Turks.

On the following page is a map showing the extent of the Turkish Empire from the beginning of the last (second) 5-month prophecy of the fifth trumpet (A.D. 1299) through a portion of the time prophecy of the sixth trumpet.

The pink and yellow territory[4] was conquered by the Turks under the second 150-year (5-month) prophecy of the fifth trumpet—A.D. 1299-1449.

---

3. The number of horsemen was two hundred thousand thousand. What this number means, expositors have been at a loss to determine. But I am inclined to believe with Mr. Miller, that it means 200,000 twice told, making 400,000 in all. What makes this probable is the fact that the Turks usually had from three to four hundred thousand horsemen in their army. They had, when Constantinople was taken, 300,000, and some say, 400,000 horsemen, besides many foot soldiers and a fleet. (Joshua V. Himes, *Signs of the Times*, vol. 1, no. 21, Feb. 1, 1841.)

4. A color version of the map may be viewed at: <http://en.wikipedia.org/wiki/History_of_the_Ottoman_Empire>.

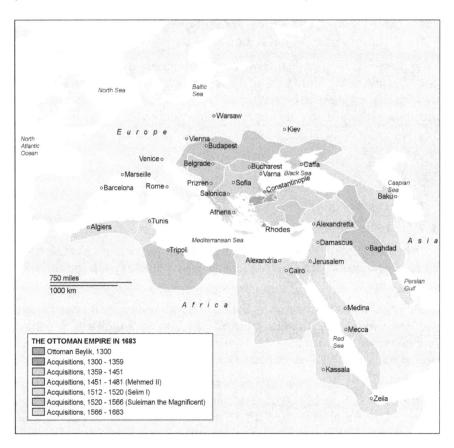

THE OTTOMAN EMPIRE IN 1683
- Ottoman Beylik, 1300
- Acquisitions, 1300 - 1359
- Acquisitions, 1359 - 1451
- Acquisitions, 1451 - 1481 (Mehmed II)
- Acquisitions, 1512 - 1520 (Selim I)
- Acquisitions, 1520 - 1566 (Suleiman the Magnificent)
- Acquisitions, 1566 - 1683

They were not able, yet, to conquer the capital, Constantinople, and destroy the Empire. Then the second woe of the sixth trumpet was poured out on Eastern Rome. The green and blue areas of the map represent the conquests of the second woe.

One of the points to identify this second-woe power was that the invading army would comprise numerous horsemen.

Historian Gibbon describes this relentless invasion:

"The *myriads of Turkish horses* overspread a frontier of 600 miles from Taurus to Azeroum and the blood of 130,000 Christians was a grateful sacrifice to the Arabian-prophet [i.e., to the Moslem religion)."[5]

---

5.   Gibbon, *Decline and Fall*, vol. VI, 252.

Red, Blue, and Yellow

Another point of identification was the color of the invaders' breast-plates and uniforms. Revelation 9:17 speaks of them as "having breast-plates of fire, and of jacinth, and brimstone." The word *jacinth* is "jacin-thine" in the Greek and denotes the color blue. Thus, when the verse speaks of "fire and jacinth and brimstone," it means red, blue, and yellow. Fire is red, jacinthine is blue, and brimstone (or sulphur) is yellow. Red, blue, and yellow—were these the colors of the uniforms of the Turkish army? Charles Daubuz, an English scholar writing of the time, says:

> "From their first appearance the Ottomans have affected to wear warlike apparel of scarlet, blue and yellow: a descriptive trait the more marked from its contrast to the military appearance of Greeks, Franks or Saracens [Arabs] who were contemporary."[6]

Yet another point of identification is that the agent that would be used to kill would be fire, smoke, and brimstone. To repeat part of our Revelation 9 passage:

> **"Thus I saw the horses . . . and the heads of the horses as the heads of lions and out of their mouths issued fire and smoke and brimstone. By these three was the third of men killed. By the fire, and by the smoke, and by the brimstone which issued out of their mouths."**—Revelation 9:17, 18.

The Siege and Fall of Constantinople

Under the first woe, the Muslims were to *torment* Eastern Rome, but under the second woe, the Muslim Turks were to *slay or kill* Eastern Rome. That meant to destroy it as a political power. To accomplish that would mean striking at the heart of the empire—the capital, which was Constantinople.

This great city had stood for 1147 years. Beginning in A.D. 626, sixteen determined attempts were made to capture this city. Only once in those sixteen attempts was anyone successful—in A.D. 1204 the fourth crusade managed to breach the walls.

In the early fifteenth century a sultan named Mahomet II ascended to the Turkish throne. He was responsible for the final destruction of Eastern Rome. His unrelenting resolve was to take Constantinople. At the age of 21, he conquered Constantinople and brought an end to the

---

6.   Charles Daubuz, quoted in Edward Bishop Elliott, *Horae Apocalyptica* (Amazon: Ulan Press, 2012), ch. VII, 508.

Byzantine Empire, absorbing its administrative apparatus into the Ottoman state. In preparation for the fulfillment of his heart's desire he studied the latest instruments of destruction with which he might bring Constantinople to its knees.

Especially did Mahomet II concentrate on gunpowder and artillery. The Turks were the first to successfully employ gunpowder in the prosecution of warfare and used it in the siege of Constantinople. This was the final "killing" or "slaying" of the Eastern Roman Empire. Uriah Smith, author of *Daniel and the Revelation,* was amazed by how the prophet John, in Revelation 9:17, 18, seemed to foresee the invention and use of gunpowder:

> "The means by which the Mohammedans achieved their wonderful conquests are described in verses 17 and 18 as fire, and smoke, and brimstone; and it is a remarkable fact that in this revolution, gun-powder was first used as an implement of war. It thus appears that John, in A.D. 96, penned a prophecy of that notable invention which appeared as a new engine of destruction thirteen hundred years from his time, and has revolutionized the mode of warfare throughout the civilized world."[7]

One cannon (see below), designed by Orban, was 27 feet long and able to hurl a 1,300-pound projectile more than a mile. This is a picture of that cannon. It took 60 oxen to haul that large cannon into position.

On April 6, 1453, Mahomet II assembled 258,000 men to commence the attack. The city was 13 miles in circumference, with 7,000 to 8,000 men to defend it.

---

7. Uriah Smith, *Synopsis of the Present Truth* (Oakland, CA: Pacific Press, 1884), 216.

Constantinople was in the form of a triangle— with the southern side protected by the Marmara Sea. The north side of the city was protected by the Bosporus Straits. The mouth of this waterway was protected by a chain. They circumvented this chain by greasing logs and pulling their ships over land to get around this chain.

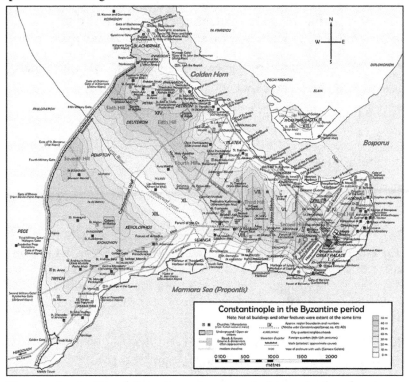

The western side of the city not connected to a body of water was protected by a double wall and a sixty-foot-wide moat, six miles long. A Turkish historian writing about the fall of Constantinople declared:

> "The Moslems placed their cannon in an effective position. The gates and ramparts of Constantinople were pierced in a thousand places. The flame which issued from the mouths of those instruments of warfare, of brazen bodies and fiery jaws, cast grief and dismay among the miscreants. The smoke which spread itself in the air rendered the brightness of day as somber as night; and the face of the world soon became as dark as the black fortune of the unhappy infidels."[8]

8.   From Saadeddin's *Diadem of Histories,* as cited by Dr. Alexander Keith in *Signs of the Times* (Edinburgh, Scotland: William Whyte & Co., 1832), bk. IV, 46.

Thus, as the prophet had declared, "by these three, by fire and smoke and brimstone was the third part of men killed." The Eastern Roman Empire was no more.

150 Years Plus a Little More Than 391 Years

The most significant point of identification regarding this second woe is in the period of time allotted "to slay the third part of men." Now, get ready for a little Bible math. The allotted time was to be for "an hour, a day, a month, and a year" (Revelation 9:15). Using the scriptural day-for-a year principle,[9] here's how that adds up:

An hour (1/24th of a day): 15 days, based on a prophetic 360-day year

A day: 1 year

A month: 30 years

A year: 360 years

TOTAL: 391 years and 15 days

In 1840 Josiah Litch, a noted preacher associated with William Miller in The Great Second Advent Movement of 1833-1844, predicted—on the basis of this time period—that the Ottoman Empire would come to its end on the 11th of August, 1840. Litch used the date of July 27, 1299 for the beginning of the five-month prophecy of the fifth trumpet, to which he added the 391 years and 15 days.

By adding the 150 years which began on July 27, 1299 to the 391 years and 15 days, Litch obtained the date of August 11, 1840.[10]

To this date, Uriah Smith would later add his agreement:

"The principal subject for exposition under this trumpet is the prophetic period brought to view in verse 15. The angels were loosed for an hour, a day, a month, and a year. This, reduced from prophetic to literal time, gives us the following period: A year, 360 days, 360 years; a month, 30 days, 30 years; a day, 1 year; an hour, a twenty-fourth part of a prophetic day, 15 literal days; making in all 391 years, and 15 days. This added to the date, July 27, 1449, where the 150 years of the previous trumpet ended, brings us to August 11, 1840."[11]

---

9.   <http://en.wikipedia.org/wiki/Day-year_principle>.

10. For an online date calendar to check out Josiah Litch's calculations (enter your own dates) go to: <http://www.timeanddate.com/date/dateadd.html>.

11. Smith, *Synopsis,* 216.

In the year 1582, a change was made from the Julian calendar to the Gregorian calendar. This change, as it happens, came midway through this prophecy. Does that throw off any calculations?

The Gregorian calendar began by dropping ten calendar days to revert to the previous date of the vernal equinox. That's why I am thankful for the online calendar calculator I've recommended in footnote 10—it takes into account the 1582 calendar change.

Prophecy Fulfilled to the *Very Day!*

So Josiah Litch's conclusion was historically correct, as far as the dates were concerned, and it was fulfilled to the very letter.

Litch confidently proclaimed to the world several months before August 11, 1840, that based on Bible prophecy, the power of the infamous Ottoman Empire would end. The world waited and watched. When it was fulfilled to the very day, a multitude of infidels were converted to the Christian faith. What a dramatic fulfillment of Litch's prediction! He had written:

"Allowing the first period, 150 years, to have been exactly fulfilled before Deacozes ascended the throne by permission of the Turks, and that the 391 years, fifteen days, commenced at the close of the first period, it will end on the 11th of August, 1840, when the Ottoman power in Constantinople may be expected to be broken. And this, I believe, will be found to be the case."[12]

At the very time specified, Turkey, through her ambassador, accepted the protection of the Allied powers of Europe and thus placed herself under the control of Christian nations. The event exactly fulfilled the prediction.

Uriah Smith wrote of the events leading up to that August 11, 1840 date:

"As the prophetic period of this [sixth] trumpet commenced by the voluntary surrender of power into the hands of the Turks by the Christian emperor of the East, so we might justly conclude that its termination would be marked by the voluntary surrender of that power by the Turkish Sultan back again into the hands of the Christians. In 1838 Turkey became involved in war with Egypt. The Egyptians bid fair to overthrow the Turkish power. To prevent this, the four great powers of Europe, England, Russia, Austria, and Prussia, interfered to sustain the Turkish government. Turkey accepted their intervention. A conference was held in London at which an ultimatum was drawn up to be

---

12. Josiah Litch, "Signs of the Times and Expositor of Prophecy," Aug. 1, 1840.

presented to Mehemet Ali, the Pacha of Egypt. It is evident that when this ultimatum should be placed in the hands of Mehemet, the destiny of the Ottoman empire would be virtually lodged in the hands of the Christian powers of Europe. *This ultimatum was placed in the hands of Mehemet on the 11th day of August 1840!* and on that very day the Sultan addressed a note to the ambassadors of the four powers, inquiring what should be done in case Mehemet refused to comply with the terms which they had proposed. The answer was that he need not alarm himself about any contingency that might arise; for they had made provision for that. The prophetic period ended, and *on that very day* the control of Mohammedan affairs passed into the hands of Christians, just as the control of Christian affairs had passed into the hands of the Mohammedans 391 years and 15 days before. Thus the second woe ended, and the sixth trumpet ceased its sounding."[13]

As we saw in our previous chapter on the first woe, the Muslims of the fifth trumpet protected the true church from the attacks of the papal armies by diverting their attention. Now, in the sixth trumpet, we have the Muslims protecting the Protestant Reformation from the assaults of the papal persecution. When the Turks were invading Europe, King Charles V of Spain was emperor of the Holy Roman Empire. Protestantism had risen in 1517, and thousands of people had left the Catholic Church to become Protestants. Charles V, being a devout Roman Catholic, was persuaded by his church not only to oppose the Protestant faith but to destroy it. But whenever he advanced to attack the Protestants, so often tidings would come that the Turks were on the attack, and Charles would be forced to turn away from the Protestants and march against the Turks. That which was a woe to the wicked was a blessing to God's people—in both the first and second woe! Might that same protection again come into play in the yet-future third woe?

Two Woes Past—One Yet Future

In our next chapter on the third woe, we will see that what we have learned from these first two woes of the past will provide insights to our understanding of what the third woe of the future will be.

Four points have been in common with each of the first two woes:

▸ The first two woes involved the Islamic caliphate.

▸ The first two woes involved warfare between Islamic and Christian nations.

---

13. Smith, *Synopsis*, 216 (emphasis supplied).

- ▶ The first two woes resulted in diverting the enemy's attention away from God's true people so they could fulfill their mission of proclaiming the gospel.

- ▶ The first two woes were redemptive scourges upon an apostate religion, designed to lead men to repentance.

As we will see in our next chapter, the third woe *also* will include all of these points. That is how we will know that we have correctly identified the third woe.

After the verses dealing with the first woe, the angel said:

"One woe is past; and, behold, there come two woes more hereafter."—Revelation 9:12.

And then, after the second woe, the angel again says:

"The second woe is past; and, behold, the third woe cometh quickly."—Revelation 11:14.

I believe this is said to show that there will be *much in common* between the three woes.

Imagine yourself now in a standing position (unless you already are!). Now imagine yourself turning exactly 180 degrees to face the opposite direction. That's what I want you to do in one sense right now. For the first two woes, you've been looking *back*—into history. For the third woe, you'll need to turn and look *forward*—into the future.

Ready? Then let's move on into chapter 6!

CHAPTER SIX

THE THIRD WOE – THE THIRD JIHAD

Let's begin our look at the third woe of Revelation with a short summary:

"And I beheld, and heard an angel flying through the midst of heaven, saying with a loud voice, Woe, woe, woe, to the inhabiters of the earth . . ."—Revelation 8:13.

Three woes. In the previous two chapters, we've focused on the first two woes of the fifth and sixth trumpets and discovered that history supports the fact that under those two trumpets, the first two Islamic Jihads took place.

▶ First woe trumpet—First Jihad: A.D. 622–750, carried out by Islamic Arabs

▶ Second woe trumpet—Second Jihad: A.D. 1071–1683, carried out by Islamic Turks

Now, note this well: Though the second great wave of Jihad may have closed in 1683, the sixth trumpet time period didn't end until the independence of the Islamic Turkish (Ottoman) Empire itself ended—in fulfillment of the prophecy of Revelation 9:15 ("an hour, and a day, and a month, and a year"—see discussion in the previous chapter). To the very day, this prophecy was fulfilled on August 11, 1840. That is the day the time period of the sixth trumpet came to an end.

"The second woe is past; and, behold, the third woe cometh quickly."—Revelation 11:14.

When did—or does—the third woe happen? Careful students of Bible prophecy around the time when the second woe ended in 1840 weren't sure just when it would happen.

Remember James White's prophecy chart of 1863 (see page 62) that described the first two woes—under images of the fifth and sixth angels sounding their trumpets—with images of a Muslim holding a spear (first woe) and a Muslim shooting a musket (second woe)? But under the third angel sounding his trumpet, White showed . . . nothing! He wasn't certain what the third woe might be—or when it would happen.

That remained the case for quite some time. But follow closely now: Increasingly, Bible students began concluding that soon after the sixth trumpet ceased to sound—and with it, the time of the second woe ended too—the seventh trumpet *began* to sound—and with it, the time of the third woe opened:

"But in the days of the voice of the seventh angel, *when he shall begin to sound* [his trumpet], the mystery of God should be finished, as he hath declared to his servants the prophets."—Revelation 10:7, emphasis supplied.

But note that in saying "the *time of* the third woe," that does not mean that this woe would necessarily take place when the time of this trumpet began. In the first woe trumpet—the fifth trumpet—centuries passed without woe. So within the time periods of the fifth, sixth, and seventh trumpet, we find woes that take place.

But first, let's "get our ducks in a row," as the saying goes. In other words, let's line up the prophetic events of Daniel and Revelation in as close to the right order as we can get them.

Let's begin with what we learned back in chapter 3—that in fulfillment of Daniel 11:45, the Islamic caliphate will be planted in Jerusalem. When? How? Why? We can't know those answers just yet, as Daniel 11:45—and the Jerusalem caliphate—are still future. But in chapter 2, we presented one possible and reasonable scenario under which the caliphate could be established in Jerusalem: We imagined the possibility of a preventive EMP (electro-magnetic pulse) strike by Israel that totally disables Iran's electronic infrastructure, rendering the nation's nuclear development and electronic infrastructure impotent. Our scenario then had a back-channel settlement involving the U.S. and Turkey, under which in exchange for Turkey's assistance in averting a full-blown nuclear World War III, Turkey would be allowed to set up a restored Islamic caliphate on Jerusalem's Mount of Olives—allowed, perhaps, because the U. S. will hope that this will finally bring peace to the Middle East.

Perhaps the conditions under which the caliphate comes to Jerusalem will involve a completely different—and at present, unforeseen and un-foreseeable—set of events. But that the "tabernacles of his palace" *will be* planted in Jerusalem is certain, backed by the unfailing prediction of Daniel 11:45.

Once planted, the newly united Islamic world will resume the same aggressive drive to expand its reach in the world, with the ultimate goal of bringing the entire globe under Islamic domination. And wherever it subdues nations, it will bring them under the control of Islamic Sharia law.

Islamic expansion—as seen in the history of the first two great Jihads—will use whatever means necessary, including military force, to extend its domain in the world.

A Jerusalem Caliphate Triggers the Third Jihad

Once the caliphate is planted in Jerusalem, the use of terrorism will be unleashed on a scale that puts 9/11 in the shade and makes it look like a minor effort. If Jihadi have at their disposal so-called "dirty bombs" that combine radioactive materials with conventional explosives, they will undoubtedly use them. If they have chemical, biological, radiologi-cal, or even limited-scale nuclear weapons of mass destruction, they will undoubtedly use them.

As this book is being published, it's been confirmed that Syria has used chemical weapons against its own people, with images of hundreds of the alleged victims available for the world to see. But after being emboldened and feeling unrestrained once a caliphate is restored, who can imagine the degree to which Jihadists may use such weapons?

The West—including the United States, Great Britain, and their al-lies—will not by any means be off-limits to Jihadic attacks. Many such attacks have already occurred, even without a caliphate. Once that piv-otal event takes place in fulfillment of Daniel 11:45, the Western na-tions will become prime targets for Islamic expansion—and the attacks will rise to a whole new level of intensity and frequency and destruc-tiveness.

To imagine thousands or even many tens of thousands of fatalities as major Western cities are attacked is not difficult. Perhaps a dirty bomb in Manhattan, a chemical attack on Los Angeles, a biological attack on Chicago or Houston.

Whatever the level of Jihadic attacks, it will be like smashing a hornet's nest with a baseball bat. The attacks will provoke the West to absolute fury. And the nations will be angry not just because of the massive destruction caused by these attacks—they will also be enraged by the imposition of Sharia law wherever Islam succeeds in subjugating nations or territories.

It's time now to return to Revelation 11 for a moment, where in verse 15 we were told of the beginning of the seventh trumpet:

> **"The second woe is past; and, behold, the third woe cometh quickly. [15]And the seventh angel sounded. . . . [18] And the nations were angry, and thy wrath is come, and the time of the dead, that they should be judged, and that thou shouldest give reward unto thy servants the prophets, and to the saints, and them that fear thy name, small and great; and shouldest destroy them which destroy the earth."**—Revelation 11:14, 15, 18.

Do you see how verse 18 began? For now, let's focus just on the first two phrases:

"And the nations were angry"

"And thy wrath is come"

Have we not just been talking about angry nations? Furious, enraged nations? And we've taken a look at the reasons, both of which follow in the train of a restored caliphate: Jihadic attacks on the West, and the imposition of Sharia law. Once the caliphate is planted in Jerusalem, the way will be prepared for the Third Jihad to commence.

Notice too in the Revelation verses above that the seventh trumpet sounding is mentioned *before* the mention of angry nations. Just as the first two Jihads/woes occurred, respectively, under the times of the fifth and sixth trumpets—but did not match exactly the trumpets' beginning and ending dates—the same is true of the Jihad/woe of the seventh trumpet. Though the time period of the seventh trumpet has already begun, the Bible suggests, since soon after 1840, the woe of this trumpet—if it is indeed a third Islamic Jihad—is yet future.

Once that Jihad begins with the planting of the caliphate in Jerusalem, events from that point forward in our earth's history occur in rapid succession and spiral into violence and chaos.

We're going to move ahead to explore that perilous time awaiting us. But just before we do, I want to note something that will throw added light on what we study together. Not long after the sixth trumpet ended in 1840, a gifted and deeply spiritual author by the name of Ellen White[1] wrote a book called *The Great Controversy,* in which she shared her own vision and conclusions—which she (and countless others since) felt certain God had opened to her mind—about the final events of this earth's history.

In the remaining pages of this chapter, I want of course to continue basing our look into the future on the prophecies of God's Word. The Bible is and always should be our primary and ultimate source for what God has to say to us. But where it can illuminate our discussion of certain future events, I'll occasionally bring in some of the key commentary from *The Great Controversy* to offer—for your consideration—a more detailed picture of what is about to happen up ahead.

If, as you read some of these comments that I'll cite here in this chapter, you are intrigued and would like to obtain a copy of this book that has found its way into untold millions of homes around the world, visit my website at: http://www.*daniel*1145.com/index.php/book-downloads —and download a free digital download or audio version, or follow the links to download a free Kindle version or purchase a printed book. (By

---

1. **"Survey Reveals The Books and Authors That Have Most Influenced Pastors**

    "May 30, 2005

    "In a remarkable report, the Barna Group, a nationally recognized polling/survey organization, recently declared Ellen White to be one of the most influential authors among a cross section of young pastors in the United States. Surveyed pastors under 40 years of age listed her as one of the top authors that impacted them personally in the last three years.

    "<https://www.barna.org/component/content/article/5-barna-update/45-barna-update-sp-657/178-survey-reveals-the-books-and-authors-that-have-most-influenced-pastors#.Vw6btfkrKHs>.

    "Ellen G. White is the most translated female non-fiction author in the history of literature, as well as the most translated American non-fiction author of either gender. . . . Her writings covered creationism, agriculture, theology, evangelism, Christian lifestyle, education and health. She advocated vegetarianism. She promoted the establishment of schools and medical centers. During her lifetime she wrote more than 5,000 periodical articles and 40 books. Today, including compilations from her 100,000 pages of manuscript, more than 100 titles are available in English. Some of her most famous books include *The Desire of Ages, The Great Controversy,* and *Steps to Christ.* Her work on successful Christian living, *Steps to Christ,* has been published in more than 140 languages." <http://en.wikipedia.org/wiki/Ellen_G._White#cite_ref-FOOTNOTEWhite2000_6-0>.

the way, on the same website page, you can download a copy of Uriah Smith's *Daniel and the Revelation,* which we've cited many times already in this book.)

Redemptive Discipline

Now, in earlier chapters, we noted that God used the first two woes as redemptive discipline on those nations and people claiming to follow Him—but had fallen into apostasy. This is one of the parallels we noted in the previous chapter—factors in common between the two woes. Why would it be any different with the third woe? It too will involve God's redemptive discipline on nations supporting apostate religion. In the United States, the chief religious system is Protestantism. Protestants at one time protested against the biblical compromises found in the Catholic Church—that's how they got their name. Biblical compromise is becoming more common within the Protestant churches of the Western nations. The eroding authority of Scripture as seen in the acceptance of evolution and the redefining of marriage are just a couple examples of unfaithfulness to the teachings of the Bible. Protestant America is in apostasy!

And God's redemptive discipline will come *through* the attacks of Islam. Yes, God will *use* them—just as in Old Testament times He so often used pagan nations to discipline His people—to discipline His people in apostate America, and other Western nations too. Without even realizing it, Islam will serve a future role as God's instrument to discipline His people enmeshed in compromised religion.

Will God get through to them? We've already noted that in response to Islamic attacks and Sharia law, the Western nations are "angry." But they are also in a state of soul-searching. Why is all this happening? Why all the death and chaos? Why has the bottom fallen out economically, plunging millions into a place far more wretched than the Great Depression?

They ask themselves: Is *God* angry? Is He in fact punishing them? And if so, what can be done?

If you're a nation that has claimed God's name but not played His game, so to speak—if you're a nation that has talked a good talk but not walked a good walk—if you have decided that anything goes, whether abortion or same-sex marriage or rampant immorality or embracing evolution— then maybe it's time to "get back to God." And how better to do that than to get people going back to church each Sunday?

Legislating Sunday Worship

As I mentioned back in chapter 2 in offering my own possible scenario of what *could* happen—based on projecting current world developments into the future—both Evangelical leaders and legislators, alarmed by national chaos and ruin, press for a law mandating required Sunday church attendance. Even the Pope warns that God's judgments are falling because people have turned their backs on Him.

People of all faiths and of, till now, no faith at all steadily conclude that something must be done to show God they mean to change their ways and return to Him. So yes, what better way than starting to go back to church each Sunday? The legislation, with wide support, easily passes.

But the national calamities don't seem to stop, so new supplemental legislation is added requiring that any who ignore the Sunday law will face punishments—among them, forfeiting the right to buy or sell, economic boycott (see Revelation 13:17).

Satan Steps In

"Woe to the inhabiters of the earth and of the sea! *for the devil is come down unto you,* **having great wrath, because he knoweth that he hath but a short time."**—Revelation 12:12, emphasis supplied.

No sooner has Sunday legislation passed, than something happens to weld the world into total unity on making Sunday worship the law. Christ appears in person to endorse it! Only it's not Christ at all—it's His enemy, Satan, impersonating Him—"the devil is come down unto you." Allow me to share how Ellen White, commenting on Revelation 12:12, envisioned this great deception in her book, *The Great Controversy:*

"As the crowning act in the great drama of deception, Satan himself will personate Christ. The church has long professed to look to the Saviour's advent as the consummation of her hopes. Now the great deceiver will make it appear that Christ has come. In different parts of the earth, Satan will manifest himself among men as a majestic being of dazzling brightness, resembling the description of the Son of God given by John in the Revelation. Revelation 1:13-15. The glory that surrounds him is unsurpassed by anything that mortal eyes have yet beheld. The shout of triumph rings out upon the air: 'Christ has come! Christ has come!' The people prostrate themselves in adoration before him, while he lifts up his hands and pronounces a blessing upon them, as Christ blessed His disciples

83

when He was upon the earth. His voice is soft and subdued, yet full of melody. In gentle, compassionate tones he presents some of the same gracious, heavenly truths which the Saviour uttered; he heals the diseases of the people, and then, in his assumed character of Christ, he claims to have changed the Sabbath to Sunday, and commands all to hallow the day which he has blessed. He declares that those who persist in keeping holy the seventh day are blaspheming his name by refusing to listen to his angels sent to them with light and truth. This is the strong, almost overmastering delusion."[2]

Did you notice that? "Jesus" (Satan) claims to have changed the biblical Sabbath to Sunday—and commands everyone to keep it holy. Of course, Satan lies—never in His time on earth did Jesus ever change the Sabbath (see Appendix G, page 141, on the Sabbath). That change was made by an apostate church centuries after His ministry on earth was done (see Appendix H, page 151, on the beast and his mark).

Once the United States has passed a strict law enforcing Sunday worship, the rest of the world is encouraged to follow suit. The law becomes universal, complete with the "no buying or selling" provision against offenders who refuse to go along. This brings the entire world to a great final test of loyalty, as to whether they will obey God and worship on the seventh-day Sabbath He created (see Genesis 2:1-3) and enshrined in His unchanging, unchangeable Ten Commandments (see Exodus 20:8-11).

Those who are loyal to God, the Bible says, will receive "the seal of God" (see Revelation 7:2, 3; 9:4). Those disloyal to Him will receive "the mark of the beast" (see Revelation 13:7; 14:9, 11: 15:2; 16:2; 19:20; and 20:4). (See Appendix H, page 151, on the mark of the beast.)

Let us move forward with our rapid overview of events.

"And the nations were angry," Revelation 11:18 said. They have responded internally by trying to show God they are changing their ways—as demonstrated in Sunday-worship legislation. Now they turn their anger outward against their attackers, determined to bring down the caliphate and the caliph who rules all Islam from his headquarters in Jerusalem.

And they succeed. Remember the prophecy?

"Yet he [the king of the north, embodied in the caliph] **shall come to his end, and none shall help him."**—Daniel 11:45.

---

2.   Ellen White, *The Great Controversy*, 624.

Four Angels Holding Back Four Winds

For only a little longer, the two clashing civilizations or religious systems are kept from totally annihilating each other—and in doing so, destroying all life on earth. How are they "kept" from this? By four mighty angels of God, who are holding back the winds of strife. Here is what the Bible says:

> **"And after these things I saw four angels standing on the four corners of the earth, holding the four winds of the earth, that the wind should not blow on the earth, nor on the sea, nor on any tree. And I saw another angel ascending from the east, having the seal of the living God: and he cried with a loud voice to the four angels, to whom it was given to hurt the earth and the sea, saying, Hurt not the earth, neither the sea, nor the trees, till we have sealed the servants of our God in their foreheads."**—Revelation 7:1-3.

These verses also give the reason for the angels' work in holding back the four winds: to allow more time for those who want to choose loyalty to God (as tested by the Sabbath-Sunday issue—see Appendix H, page 151) and receive His seal in their foreheads. That seal—as we noted in chapter 4—is the seventh-day Sabbath of the fourth commandment of God's law ("seal the law among my disciples."—Isaiah 8:16).

Finally, though, all who are going to choose have chosen—either to be loyal to God, or to reject His Sabbath and give their allegiance to a manmade Sabbath. Only God will know when that time has come, but when it has, Jesus Christ will finish His work in heaven, applying His blood on behalf of those who have chosen Him—and He will "stand up":

> **"And at that time shall Michael** [Jesus] **stand up, the great prince which standeth for the children of thy people . . ."**—Daniel 12:1.

Human probation—the opportunity to choose for God or against Him—is at an end. Probation has closed for the human race. This is when Jesus acknowledges that wherever anyone is in their allegiance or non-allegiance to God, is where they will stay. Each person has "locked in" his or her choice. Jesus proclaims:

> **"He that is unjust, let him be unjust still: and he which is filthy, let him be filthy still: and he that is righteous, let him be righteous still: and he that is holy, let him be holy still."**—Revelation 22:11.

With probation closed, the world has reached an awful time. A time the Bible calls "a time of trouble." Let's read the entire verse in Daniel 12:1:

"And at that time shall Michael stand up, the great prince which standeth for the children of thy people: and there shall be *a time of trouble, such as never was* since there was a nation even to that same time: and at that time thy people shall be delivered, every one that shall be found written in the book"—emphasis supplied.

Redemptive Discipline Turns to Retributive Punishment: "And thy wrath is come"

Note this now: *Before* the close of probation, God's *redemptive discipline* will be directed primarily toward those who still have time to choose to be His followers. This discipline will be meted out at the hands of Islam in its determined efforts to subdue the Western nations.

But "the time of trouble such as never was" is *after* the close of probation. Efforts on God's part to be redemptive would now be futile—everyone has already made a final choice. Instead, what happens next is God's "wrath is come"—His *retributive punishment* or justice on those who have forever turned against Him. The trouble now to come on the earth and on those frozen in rebellion against God—sometimes referred to as "the wicked"—is almost too horrific to describe or imagine. But it's right there in the Bible—in Revelation 16. Here we read of a series of ghastly catastrophes to fall in swift succession on the earth—the Bible calls them the seven last plagues. In brief, these plagues are:

▶ First: Grievous sores (Revelation 16:2)

▶ Second: Sea becomes as blood of a dead man (verse 3)

▶ Third: The rivers and fountains of waters also become blood (verse 4)

▶ Fourth: The sun scorches men with fire (verse 8)

▶ Fifth: Seat of the beast is filled with darkness and pain and sores (verse 10)

▶ Sixth: The River Euphrates is dried up, preparing the way for the kings of the east; unclean spirits of devils working miracles go out to gather the nations to the Battle of Armageddon (verses 12-16)

▶ Seventh: A voice from heaven's temple says, "It is done"; a massive earthquake strikes; islands and mountains disappear; huge hailstones fall (verses 17-21)

These seven last plagues will plunge this earth into its final convulsions. Those who take the shelter that will be described in the next chapter of this book will be spared these plagues. The Bible promises protection to the faithful:

"A thousand shall fall at thy side, and ten thousand at thy right hand; but it shall not come nigh thee."—Psalm 91:7.

"Because thou hast made the LORD, which is my refuge, even the most High, thy habitation; there shall no evil befall thee, neither shall any plague come nigh thy dwelling."—Psalm 91:9, 10.

Yes, contrary to a popular and erroneous belief, followers of God will not be raptured away to escape this time of trouble. No, they will be still be here living in their dwellings, as Psalm 91:10 states. But the plagues cannot touch them, because of the shelter they have taken—the protection that God provides.

Plague Number Six: Armageddon

I want now to turn attention to the final two plagues—the sixth and the seventh. Plague number six is the gathering together of the world to the great final Battle of Armageddon.

After the devastating terrorist attacks on its own homeland, the United States is looking for payback. In this, they are joined by other Western nations which, too, have suffered massive destruction and casualties.

And after the caliphate has been taken down, the world of Islam is also looking for payback.

Remember that probation has now closed. The angels holding back the "winds of war" have now released their hold. Nothing stands in the way of the determination by both sides to seek revenge. Many scores demand to be settled—many grievances call for forceful action. And Satan now has full control of those who have sided against God and failed His test of loyalty—the observance of God's holy day, the seventh-day Sabbath of the fourth commandment.

So it will be, says Revelation 16, that the two great clashing and contending civilizations marshal their forces for one final "war to end all wars." Russia, China, and the axis of Islamic nations that hate the Judeo-Christian West will possibly unite, determined to bring a final solution. For its part, the West will be just as united and determined. No holds will be barred. The Geneva Conventions and all other wartime conventions will be trashed. The nations of the earth will unite to wage one final battle described by the sixth plague of Revelation 16—Armageddon:

> **"And the sixth angel poured out his vial upon the great river Euphrates; and the water thereof was dried up, that the way of the kings of the east might be prepared. And I saw three unclean spirits like frogs come out of the mouth of the dragon, and out of the mouth of the beast, and out of the mouth of the false prophet. For they are the spirits of devils, working miracles, which go forth unto the kings of the earth and of the whole world, to** *gather them to the battle of that great day of God Almighty.* **Behold, I come as a thief. Blessed is he that watcheth, and keepeth his garments, lest he walk naked, and they see his shame.** *And he gathered them together into a place called in the Hebrew tongue Armageddon."*—Revelation 16:12-16, emphasis supplied.

Now, there's a lot in these verses that we could dwell on—kings of the east, three unclean spirits, spirits of devils . . . But for now, let's focus in on the fact that under the sixth angel, the sixth of the seven last plagues will lead to the Battle of Armageddon.

A Death Decree

Meanwhile, as events quickly escalate toward a final battle, the fury of those who have rejected God intensifies. God's faithful ones are blamed for the chaos and rage seen everywhere. After all, these are the ones who are standing in the way of gaining God's favor by the legislating of Sunday worship. First came the law mandating Sunday worship attendance. Later, a penalty was added for violators—they could no longer buy or sell. But now, the nations have "had it" with the small—and as it is seen, stubborn—group of holdouts. No more tolerance. What happens next, I'll share through the pen of Ellen White:

> "As the Sabbath has become the special point of controversy throughout Christendom, and religious and secular authorities have combined to enforce the observance of the Sunday, the persistent refusal of a small minority to yield to the popular demand will make them objects of universal execration. It will be urged that the few who stand in opposition to an institution of the church and a law of the state ought not to be tolerated; that it is better for them to suffer than for whole nations to be thrown into confusion and lawlessness. The same argument eighteen hundred years ago was brought against Christ by the 'rulers of the people.' 'It is expedient for us,' said the wily Caiaphas, 'that one man should die for the people, and

that the whole nation perish not.' John 11:50. This argument will appear conclusive; and *a decree will finally be issued against those who hallow the Sabbath of the fourth commandment, denouncing them as deserving of the severest punishment and giving the people liberty, after a certain time, to put them to death.* Romanism in the Old World and apostate Protestantism in the New will pursue a similar course toward those who honor all the divine precepts."[3]

I personally would not be surprised if about this same time, the same enemy of God who impersonated His Second Coming were to persuade the world's leaders that this raging battle—and the ongoing seven final plagues, with the potential annihilation of the human race—cannot be stopped unless the Sabbath keepers are put to death.

The Time of Jacob's Trouble

The death decree is issued, and this plunges God's faithful people into a time of trouble *within* the worldwide time of trouble. This "time of Jacob's trouble," many Bible students are convinced, was foreseen by Jeremiah:

> **"Alas! for that day is great, so that none is like it: it is even the time of Jacob's trouble, but he shall be saved out of it."**—Jeremiah 30:7.

This Scripture is alluding to the story of Jacob's all night fight for his life, described in Genesis 32. Jacob was in big trouble. His brother, with an army of 400 men, was marching toward his defenseless family. His sin of deceiving his brother many years earlier now resulted in things looking as if he were about to pay for that sin with his life. He was praying for protection, when suddenly, he was attacked by an unknown assailant. He wrestled all night with a divine being whom he at first believed to be an enemy. Jacob prevailed and was given a new name—Israel. And God delivered him from the sword of his brother.

Unseen to these faithful ones at the end of time, a spirited battle—both literal and spiritual—rages between good and evil angels and wicked men on earth. Will God deliver them? We'll discover the answer just a few paragraphs ahead.

Armageddon Halted

Whether the battle reaches a point where conventional warfare is abandoned and both sides plan—or even begin to use—nuclear weapons, we

---

3.   White, *The Great Controversy*, 615, 615, emphasis supplied.

just don't know. But here is what we *do* know, based on Scripture. Before things can get really out of hand, the battle is interrupted—brought to a total and abrupt halt. The attention of the entire world will be focused on God, who speaks out of His temple of heaven. The seventh angel pours out the seventh and final plague:

> **"And the seventh angel poured out his vial into the air; and there came *a great voice out of the temple of heaven, from the throne, saying, It is done.* And there were voices, and thunders, and lightnings; and there was a great earthquake, such as was not since men were upon the earth, so mighty an earthquake, and so great. And the great city was divided into three parts, and the cities of the nations fell: and great Babylon came in remembrance before God, to give unto her the cup of the wine of the fierceness of his wrath. And every island fled away, and the mountains were not found. And there fell upon men a great hail out of heaven, every stone about the weight of a talent: and men blasphemed God because of the plague of the hail; for the plague thereof was exceeding great."**—Revelation 16:17-21, emphases supplied.

Notice some of what this verse says now happens:

▸ A voice (God's voice) is heard from heaven, saying "It is done."

▸ Voices, lightnings, and thunders are seen and heard.

▸ The greatest earthquake in human history strikes the world.

▸ The islands flee away; the mountains are leveled.

The seventh plague reaches its climactic finish with a plague of huge hailstones, each weighing about "a talent," or around 50 pounds each.

Human beings spurred on by Satan are no longer in control of this world—God is. And His retributive justice is now unleashed on the unrepentant rebels of this earth. Again, let's look at how Ellen White described the verses above from Revelation 16:

> "It is at midnight that God manifests His power for the deliverance of His people. The sun appears, shining in its strength. Signs and wonders follow in quick succession. The wicked look with terror and amazement upon the scene, while the righteous behold with solemn joy the tokens of their deliverance. Everything in nature seems turned out of its course. The streams cease to flow. Dark, heavy clouds come up and clash against each other. In the midst of the angry heavens is one clear space of indescribable glory, whence

comes the voice of God like the sound of many waters, saying: 'It is done.' Revelation 16:17. That voice shakes the heavens and the earth. There is a mighty earthquake, 'such as was not since men were upon the earth, so mighty an earthquake, and so great.' Verses 17, 18. The firmament appears to open and shut. The glory from the throne of God seems flashing through. The mountains shake like a reed in the wind, and ragged rocks are scattered on every side. There is a roar as of a coming tempest. The sea is lashed into fury. There is heard the shriek of a hurricane like the voice of demons upon a mission of destruction. The whole earth heaves and swells like the waves of the sea. Its surface is breaking up. Its very foundations seem to be giving way. Mountain chains are sinking. Inhabited islands disappear. The seaports that have become like Sodom for wickedness are swallowed up by the angry waters. Babylon the great has come in remembrance before God, 'to give unto her the cup of the wine of the fierceness of His wrath.' Great hailstones, every one 'about the weight of a talent,' are doing their work of destruction. Verses 19, 21. The proudest cities of the earth are laid low."[4]

Time Ends; Eternity Begins—the Second Coming of Jesus

Soon, the voice from heaven speaks again, this time announcing the very day and hour of the Second Coming of Jesus:

"The voice of God is heard from heaven, declaring the day and hour of Jesus' coming, and delivering the everlasting covenant to His people. Like peals of loudest thunder His words roll through the earth. The Israel of God stand listening, with their eyes fixed upward. Their countenances are lighted up with His glory, and shine as did the face of Moses when he came down from Sinai. The wicked cannot look upon them. And when the blessing is pronounced on those who have honored God by keeping His Sabbath holy, there is a mighty shout of victory.

"Soon there appears in the east a small black cloud, about half the size of a man's hand. It is the cloud which surrounds the Saviour and which seems in the distance to be shrouded in darkness. The people of God know this to be the sign of the Son of man. In solemn silence they gaze upon it as it draws nearer the earth, becoming lighter and more glorious, until it is a great white cloud, its base a glory like consuming fire, and above it the rainbow of the covenant. Jesus rides forth as a mighty conqueror. Not now a 'Man of Sorrows,' to

---

4.   White, *The Great Controversy*, 636.

drink the bitter cup of shame and woe, He comes, victor in heaven and earth, to judge the living and the dead. 'Faithful and True,' 'in righteousness He doth judge and make war.' And 'the armies which were in heaven' (Revelation 19:11, 14) follow Him. With anthems of celestial melody the holy angels, a vast, unnumbered throng, attend Him on His way. The firmament seems filled with radiant forms— 'ten thousand times ten thousand, and thousands of thousands.' No human pen can portray the scene; no mortal mind is adequate to conceive its splendor. 'His glory covered the heavens, and the earth was full of His praise. And His brightness was as the light.' Habakkuk 3:3, 4. As the living cloud comes still nearer, every eye beholds the Prince of life. No crown of thorns now mars that sacred head; but a diadem of glory rests on His holy brow. His countenance outshines the dazzling brightness of the noonday sun. 'And He hath on His vesture and on His thigh a name written, King of kings, and Lord of lords.' Revelation 19:16."[5]

The long, horrific nightmare of sin—with all the misery and pain and tears and death it has brought to this world—is over. Forever gone. Jesus has made good on His promise to return to this world and take His faithful people with Him to their new home in heaven. Then, after a thousand years, says Revelation 20, He will bring them back to this earth and re-create it in total perfection. The New Earth will be the home of the saved, where they will live in perfect peace and joy for all eternity.

Are We Prepared?

What a future can be ours! But are we ready for what lies between now and eternity on a New Earth? Are we ready for the last convulsive events still ahead of us? Ready for more trouble than this world has ever seen? Ready for economic ruin, for horrendous attacks right here in America and in other Western nations, for persecution when we choose to follow God instead of man-made rules?

How can we BE ready? That is what we'll ask—and answer—in the next and final chapter of this book.

5.　White, *The Great Controversy*, 640, 641.

CHAPTER SEVEN

ARE YOU PREPARED?

Not that long ago, most of us had never even heard the word *prepper*. But that was then—and this is now. Consider this:

- ▶ Now, after several seasons, *Doomsday Preppers*—a reality TV series on National Geographic—is that channel's most-watched and highest-rated series ever.

- ▶ *Doomsday Castle,* first an episode on *Doomsday Preppers,* is now its own series on the National Geographic Channel, featuring the lives of Brenton Bruns and his ten children, preparing for the end of the world in a castle he has built in South Carolina.

- ▶ The Discovery Channel recently aired a special titled *Apocalypse Preppers,* which took a look at the "mind-boggling ways" that people are preparing for the end of the world—which some see as a foregone conclusion and not just a possibility.

- ▶ You can know that a cultural phenomenon has become widespread, when one website features an article entitled "Rise of the Preppers: 50 of the Best Prepper Websites and Blogs on the Internet."[1] That's far from ALL such sites—but simply a selection of "50 of the Best."

- ▶ One such website says: "It is estimated that there are at least two

---

1. <http://www.shtfplan.com/emergency-preparedness/rise-of-the-preppers-50-of-the-best-prepper-websites-and-blogs-on-the-internet_02012013>.

million preppers in the United States today, but nobody really knows."[2] Another site says three million.[3]

▸ Preppers, or survivalists, are concerned about everything from possible economic collapse, to crippling natural disasters, catastrophic earth changes, the "Big Brother" surveillance grid, terrorism, killer pandemics, EMP (electromagnetic pulse) attacks, World War III, solar megastorms, asteroid strikes, and total societal chaos.

▸ Preppers "prepare" in different ways and to different degrees. Some stockpile food, supplies, and weaponry. Some build remote bunkers. Some buy gold and other precious metals. Many try to relocate from urban to rural areas and "get back to the land." Most are working at downsizing their belongings, getting out of debt, and learning how to grow their own food.

No one can successfully challenge the fact that our nation—and our world—seems to be accelerating toward something that will cause great trouble, if not outright catastrophe. Recent political brinksmanship shows that the risk of a major economic collapse, even to the point of a new Great Depression, is very real. The natural world is running out of critical resources. And natural disasters can be demonstrated to be increasing in frequency and destructiveness. Over all of this looms the darkening cloud of terrorism and a renewed post–Cold War nuclear threat.

As author of this book, I am among those who believe in becoming prepared for whatever is coming on this world. I may not be huddled in fear and paranoia in a backwoods bunker somewhere guarding my stash of gold bullion with an AK-47 across my lap, but I think that taking steps toward preparedness is the only common-sense course I can take, given the warning signs that this world is headed for unprecedented trouble. Cutting down possessions, becoming self-sufficient, assembling some emergency supplies, getting finances in order—these things I believe we should all be doing.

My own personal "prepping" isn't motivated just by the daily headlines I hear and read. Far more, it's based on the prediction we've already found in earlier chapters, that is set to occur not long from now:

"And there shall be a time of trouble, such as never was since there was a nation even to that same time."—Daniel 12:1.

A time of trouble such as never was before! Yes, that time IS coming—

2. <http://preppercentral.com>.
3. <http://www.shtfplan.com>.

and soon. And if we think for a moment that things in our world are in bad shape now, we haven't seen anything yet!

The urgent question, then, is what can we do to prepare? How can we be ready? We've already looked at what Revelation chapter 16 says about seven last great plagues that will fall on this earth. Let's consider just the first one for a moment: a "noisome and grievous sore." Whatever that is, it's going to be painful. Listen to this:

"And they gnawed their tongues for pain, and blasphemed the God of heaven because of their pains and their sores"—Revelation 16:10, 11.

How can preppers—how can any of us—find protection from this first horrific plague? The answer is in the text itself. Notice:

"And I heard a great voice out of the temple saying to the seven angels, Go your ways, and pour out the vials of the wrath of God upon the earth. And the first went, and poured out his vial upon the earth; and there fell a noisome and grievous sore upon the men *which had the mark of the beast, and upon them which worshipped his image.*"—Revelation 16:1, 2, emphasis supplied.

There's only one way to avoid this first plague and the six that follow and that is to not receive the mark of the beast or worship his image. In fact, making sure we don't receive this mark is so important that God sent three angels with three messages of warning, and if we heed these three messages, we will not receive this mark of the beast. Here is the third angel's message that warns against this mark:

"And the third angel followed them, saying with a loud voice, If any man worship the beast and his image, and receive his mark in his forehead, or in his hand, The same shall drink of the wine of the wrath of God, which is poured out without mixture into the cup of his indignation; and he shall be tormented with fire and brimstone in the presence of the holy angels, and in the presence of the Lamb: And the smoke of their torment ascendeth up for ever and ever: and they have no rest day nor night, who worship the beast and his image, and whosoever receiveth the mark of his name. Here is the patience of the saints: here are they that keep the commandments of God, and the faith of Jesus."—Revelation 14:9-12.

Preppers, let me speak to you for a moment. Are you serious about preparing for the future? Your stocked-to the-hilt country bunkers and AK-47s are not going to cut it when it comes to the wrath of God. Your only protection will be found in what Revelation 14:12 says:

- ▸ Saintly patience
- ▸ Keeping God's commandments
- ▸ Having the faith of Jesus

Those who do this are not going to receive the mark of the beast. What is this mark? Who is this beast? Good questions that *do* have answers from the Bible (see the Appendix H, page 151, for more information on the beast and his mark). But even if you couldn't figure out the answers, don't worry, you will not receive this dreaded mark if you are a patient saint keeping the commandments of God and living out the faith of Jesus.

So let's be patient saints. Yes, easier said than done, right? Let me share something intensely personal with you.

In earlier years, patience was not my hallmark. I had a hair-trigger temper and could not control my anger. I also had addictions that I couldn't kick. I couldn't keep the commandments of God if my life depended on it. I was "accustomed to do evil," and there was nothing I could do to change that. The prophet Jeremiah summed it up well, when he wrote:

> **"Can the Ethiopian change his skin, or the leopard his spots? then may ye also do good, that are accustomed to do evil?"**—Jeremiah 13:23.

But I truly *wanted* to be patient. I *wanted* to do good. I *wanted* to keep the commandments of God. However, for me this would be as impossible to do as it would be for the leopard to change his spots. Paul described my condition perfectly:

> **"For I know that in me (that is, in my flesh), dwelleth no good thing: for to will is present with me; but how to perform that which is good I find not. For the good that I would I do not: but the evil which I would not, that I do."**—Romans 7: 18, 19.

To my great relief, God had a remedy for my situation, and I found it in that little phrase at the very end of the third angel's message—"the faith of Jesus" (see Appendix I, page 167, for an explanation of this phrase, *the faith of Jesus*).

I have discovered by experience that when I keep the faith of Jesus, God works a miracle of grace in my life, giving me a new heart and writing His law within this heart, as He promised to do in Ezekiel and Jeremiah:

> **"A new heart also will I give you, and a new spirit will I put**

within you: and I will take away the stony heart out of your flesh, and I will give you an heart of flesh. And I will put my spirit within you, and cause you to walk in my statutes, and ye shall keep my judgments, and do them."—Ezekiel 36:26, 27.

"But this shall be the covenant that I will make with the house of Israel; after those days, saith the LORD, I will put my law in their inward parts, and write it in their hearts; and will be their God, and they shall be my people."—Jeremiah 31:33.

I could see that this would work! If God's law could be written in my mind, and if He would cause me to walk in obedience to His commandments, then obedience would be completely a work of His divine grace. If He didn't do it, it wasn't going to happen.

And this all came to me as a complete gift. I couldn't do anything to earn or merit this miracle of a changed life—yet to take possession of this free gift, it cost me everything I had.

Does this all sound a bit confusing? Sure it does, but hang tight; you'll see in a moment what I'm talking about. Jesus gave His disciples the following illustration:

"Again, the kingdom of heaven is like unto treasure hid in a field; the which when a man hath found, he hideth, and for joy thereof goeth and selleth all that he hath, and buyeth that field."—Matthew 13:44.

So the treasure is free but we can't have it unless we first purchase the field. And that field will cost us absolutely everything we've got.

The incredible thing about this is that everyone has exactly what it takes to buy this field. We have the right currency required to make this purchase. And what is this currency? A sin-polluted heart—my hot temper, my lustful and selfish thoughts, my carnal entertainment choices, my foul language, my dishonest conduct—I will spare you the rest of my list. We all have our list of besetting sins—some we don't like and some we cherish.

I had just enough "money" to buy the field if I gave all—my sin-polluted heart with its commandment-breaking ways. This is what repentance is all about—surrendering "all that he hath". If I had decided to hold on to even one small vice, I wouldn't have had enough "money" to buy the field and without having title to the field I couldn't have taken possession of this amazing gift of grace, the treasure of Christ Jesus Himself.

Paul summed it up in his letter to the Ephesians:

"For by grace are ye saved through faith; and that not of yourselves: it is the gift of God: Not of works, lest any man should boast. For we are his workmanship, created in Christ Jesus unto good works, which God hath before ordained that we should walk in them."—Ephesians 2:8-10.

And this grace came to me by faith—by the faith of Jesus; by faith *in* Jesus! And it can come to you too. I don't care if you are a Muslim, Jew, Atheist, Hindu, Buddhist, Catholic, or Protestant; you must have this same grace that comes through the faith of Jesus if you want to be a transformed person who will be a patient saint, keeping the commandments of God.

Remember, these are the only ones who will not receive the mark of the beast and thus be sheltered from the seven last plagues.

Untold millions have accepted this free gift of grace and have found shelter for the coming storm, no matter how fiercely it may rage. I urge you, reader, please—while you have time and things are still comparatively peaceful—take this gift that was purchased by the Son of God upon the Cross of Calvary.

Listen to the appeal Jesus Himself made:

"For God so loved the world, that he gave his only begotten Son, that whosoever believeth in him should not perish, but have everlasting life. For God sent not his Son into the world to condemn the world; but that the world through him might be saved."—John 3:16, 17.

Accepting Jesus as your Lord and Savior and in doing so, placing yourself under His protection, is the only safe shelter for the time of trouble that is about to strike our planet as an overwhelming surprise.

When the whole world is in chaos and filled with great danger, you can be safe—the Bible says you will be safe—if you choose Jesus as your Protector. Notice what He promises:

"For in the time of trouble he shall hide me in his pavilion: in the secret of his tabernacle shall he hide me; he shall set me up upon a rock."—Psalms 27:5.

"He that dwelleth in the secret place of the most High shall abide under the shadow of the Almighty. I will say of the LORD, He is my refuge and my fortress: my God; in him will I trust. Surely he shall deliver thee from the snare of the fowler, and from the noisome pestilence. He shall cover thee with his feathers, and under his wings shalt thou trust: his truth shall be thy

shield and buckler. Thou shalt not be afraid for the terror by night; nor for the arrow that flieth by day; Nor for the pestilence that walketh in darkness; nor for the destruction that wasteth at noonday. A thousand shall fall at thy side, and ten thousand at thy right hand; but it shall not come nigh thee. Only with thine eyes shalt thou behold and see the reward of the wicked. Because thou hast made the LORD, which is my refuge, even the most High, thy habitation; There shall no evil befall thee, neither shall any plague come nigh thy dwelling."—Psalms 91:1-10.

There you have it – a pavilion, a bunker, a refuge that will provide complete protection for what's coming. The wrath of God that will be poured out on the rebellious through the seven last plagues *will not touch you,* because you will have the seal of God rather than the mark of the beast.

In previous chapters, we noted that in Islam's first two great Jihads, God seemed quite clearly to use these Jihads to visit punishment and judgment on nations supporting apostate religions. The Third Jihad soon to come will also fulfill a similar role.

Another point of commonality between the first two woes (see chapter 5) was that the woes resulted in diverting the enemy's attention away from God's true people so they could fulfill their mission of proclaiming the gospel. How does this identifying commonality between the three Jihads play out during the time of the third woe?

Here's how: Islam provides protection to God's people as they give to the world its final appeals and warning messages in Revelation 18, by diverting authorities in power from stopping those who are giving this final call. Why? Because their attention is focused on the Islamic Third Jihad that is ravaging the nations. This will provide time and space to those giving the final warning message of Revelation 18:

"And after these things I saw another angel come down from heaven, having great power; and the earth was lightened with his glory. And he cried mightily with a strong voice, saying, Babylon the great is fallen, is fallen, and is become the habitation of devils, and the hold of every foul spirit, and a cage of every unclean and hateful bird. For all nations have drunk of the wine of the wrath of her fornication, and the kings of the earth have committed fornication with her, and the merchants of the earth are waxed rich through the abundance of her delicacies. And I heard another voice from heaven, saying, Come out of her, my people, that ye be not partakers of her sins, and that ye receive not of her plagues."—Revelation 18:1-4.

Before the seven plagues are poured out, before the close of proba-tion, a final invitation is given to the world to enter the "ark" of safety, so to speak. In the days of Noah, when the animals went into the ark, this supernatural event should have caught the attention of the antediluvians. The "animals climbing aboard the ark" for these last days will be seen in the amazing, unexpected fulfillment of the prophecy of Daniel 11:45 and the universal Sunday law that follows. When these events take place, the entire world will be brought to a final test. Will we obey the law of God—or the law of man? This will be a test of loyalty similar to the test that Adam and Eve were given at the very beginning of this earth's history.

The fourth commandment, unlike the other commandments, may ap-pear to us as somewhat arbitrary. Why shouldn't God be just as happy if we decide to choose a different day to keep holy? Could it be that the seventh-day Sabbath is a test of loyalty? Does God have the authority to write the rules? God told Adam and Eve to not eat from one particular tree. That may have seemed somewhat arbitrary, but that is what made it such a good test of loyalty. If someone came along and told them that all trees were alike before the Lord—that they could eat from any tree in the garden just as long as they left one tree of their own choosing alone—they would know that he was God's enemy. We don't have a tree from which we are told not to eat. Instead, we have a specific day that we are commanded to remember to keep holy. Why? Because God said to—and if we love and respect our Creator, that alone ought to be reason enough.

Reader, you don't have to wait until "the animals go into the ark." God wants you to respond to Him today. He is calling you to come out of Babylon—those religious systems that pervert the Word of God, that deny the sacrifice of the Son of God, and that belittle God's seventh-day Sabbath. He is calling you to unite with those patient saints who *keep* the commandments of God and the faith of Jesus.

God doesn't just call His people out of Babylon; He also calls them to unite with His fold:

"And other sheep I have, which are not of this fold: them also I must bring, and they shall hear my voice; and there shall be one fold, and one shepherd."—John 10:16.

If you seek for God and His truth, He will lead you to His fold. Just look for those people who are honoring the seventh-day Sabbath and who are looking for the Second Coming of Jesus, while giving the three angel's messages of Revelation 14 throughout the world.

In this chapter, and in this book, we've carefully studied the prophecies of the Bible's two great prophetic books that look forward from where we are today—to the events that are about to occur between now and when Jesus comes back to this earth.

We've seen how Daniel, chapter 11, and particularly verse 45, points to the establishment of the Islamic caliphate in Jerusalem. We've seen how two great Islamic Jihads have already occurred in history—and how a restored caliphate and Third Jihad are part of Islam's plan to bring the entire world under Islamic rule and sharia law.

We've seen from the Bible that a great and terrible time of trouble is about to break on our world, and that this time of trouble will include seven great plagues from God in heaven, including the great final Battle of Armageddon, culminating in the Second Coming of Jesus.

We've seen both history's record and Bible prophecies and placed them side-by-side with current events in America, in Europe, in the Middle East, in the entire Islamic world—and we've seen how prophecies line right up with today's headlines and the trend of events as we can best project them into the future.

We've seen and we sense that something truly earth-shaking and earth-changing is about to happen—and we know that in at least some ways, the preppers are right—we simply *must* get ready for whatever is coming.

But while preparing physically and financially is important, the only preparation that can truly see us through what lies ahead is to prepare ourselves spiritually. That means investing intensely in getting to know Jesus Christ—in spending time in His Word and in daily, even hourly communication with Him through prayer.

Those who do this will have His faith—and will have faith in Him. They will be safe under His protection, no matter the strength of the hurricane-force winds of trouble that may blow furiously all around them. They will be peaceful on the inside, filled with anticipation of the nearness of that moment when they will see their Savior and Lord face to face as He descends in unimaginable glory at His Second Coming.

My reading friend, I want—and plan—to be among those who spend eternity with Jesus on a new and sin-free earth, with its capital city, the New Jerusalem, in present-day Palestine. Our lives will be lived in perfect happiness and peace, forever and ever.

We don't have much time left to make our choice for Jesus and against all the false "religions" of this world. Have you brought your sins to Jesus yet for Him to forgive? Have you invited Him to come in and live His life in you every day and hour? If not, why not now?

Yes. *Why not now?* Jesus is waiting with open arms to welcome you!

A Personal Bible Tutor

The Ethiopian Finance Minister in the 8th chapter of Acts was having a hard time understanding Bible prophecy until Philip came along and offered to assist him. There may be a Philip who can help you too. A personal Bible Tutor can sit down with you in your home to help you better understand the Bible.

Check for availability in your area at:

www.BibleTutor.org

Find Answers to Life's Questions

Not sure where to turn? Send in your question and our Bibleinfo team will help you find your answer.

www.Bibleinfo.com

HISTORY OF THE MIDDLE EAST CONFLICT

**Middle East Conflict From 539 B.C. to the End of Time
An Interpretation of Daniel II:I Through Daniel 12:I**

1. **Also I** (Gabriel) **in the first year** (539/538 B.C.) **of Darius the Mede, even I, stood to confirm and to strengthen him** (Darius the Mede).

2. **And now will I** (Gabriel) **show thee the truth** (a term Gabriel uses when he is going to speak in plain language). **Behold** (after Cyrus)**, there shall stand up yet** (or reign) **three kings in Persia** (Cambyses, son of Cyrus 530-522; Smerdis, 522; and Darius Hystaspes, 522-486)**; and the fourth** (Xerxes—the Ahasuerus of Esther, 486-465) **shall be far richer than they all: and by his** (Xerxes) **strength through his riches he shall stir up all against the realm of Grecia** (480 B.C.)**.**

3. **And a mighty king** (Alexander the Great, 336-323) **shall stand up, that shall rule with great dominion, and do** (with the Persian kings) **according to his will.**

4. **And when he** (Alexander) **shall stand up, his kingdom shall be broken** (Alexander died in 323 B.C.)**, and shall be divided toward the four winds of heaven; and not to his** (Alexander's) **posterity, nor according to his** (Alexander's)

dominion which he (Alexander) ruled: for his (Alexander's) kingdom shall be plucked up, even for others besides those. (By 301 B.C., Alexander's kingdom was divided into four parts by his generals, who eventually killed Philip, his half-brother, and his posthumous son, Aegus. Cassander ruled Macedonia; Lysimachus ruled Thrace and Asia Minor; Seleucus ruled from Syria to the river Indus; and Ptolemy ruled Egypt and Palestine.)

5. And the king of the south (Ptolemy I Soter, 323-282, of Egypt) shall be strong, and one of his (Ptolemy I Soter's) princes (Seleucus I Nicator, who became the Syrian king of the north); and he (Seleucus I) shall be strong above him (Ptolemy I), and have dominion; his (Seleucus I's) dominion shall be a great dominion (Seleucus ruled a Greek Empire that stretched from Syria to India).

6. And in the end of years (thirty-five years after the death of Seleucus I in 281, which brings us to 246 B.C.) they (Seleucus of Syria and Ptolemy of Egypt) shall join themselves together; for the king's daughter of the south (Bernice, daughter of Ptolemy II Philadelphus) shall come to the king of the north to make an agreement (Bernice married Antiochus II Theos, who divorced Laodice to do so): but she (Bernice) shall not retain the power of the arm (Antiochus reconciled with Laodice after Bernice had a son); neither shall he (Antiochus II) stand (Laodice poisoned Antiochus II), nor his (Antiochus II's) arm (Antiochus' son by Bernice was killed): but she (Bernice) shall be given up, and they (Bernice's maids) that brought her (Bernice and her maids of honor were all killed by Laodice), and he (Ptolemy II) that begat her (Ptolemy II died; some texts read "begotten of her"; if so, it refers to her son, who was killed by Laodice), and he (Antiochus II) that strengthened her (Bernice) in these times (another reference to Antiochus II, who was killed by Laodice).

7. But out of a branch (sibling) of her (Bernice's) roots shall one (Ptolemy III Euergetes, brother of Bernice) stand up in his (Ptolemy II's) estate (Egypt), which shall come with an army, and shall enter into the fortress (Syria) of the king of the north (Seleucus II of Syria), and shall deal against them (the Syrians), and shall prevail (in 246 B.C., Ptolemy II successfully invaded Syria to take revenge on the death of his sister):

8. **And shall also carry captives into Egypt their** (Egypt's) **gods** (Ptolemy retrieved images of their gods that Cambyses of Persia had taken away)**, with their princes, and with their precious vessels of silver and of gold; and he** (Ptolemy III) **shall continue more years than the king of the north** (Ptolemy III outlived Seleucus II by four years).

9. **So the king of the south** (Ptolemy Euergetes) **shall come into his kingdom** (Seleucus II Callinicus)**, and shall return into his** (Ptolemy Euergetes) **own land** (if Ptolemy had not been recalled into Egypt by a domestic sedition, he would have possessed the whole kingdom of Seleucus).

10. **But his** (Seleucus II's) **sons** (Seleucus III Ceraunus Soter, 225-223, and Antiochus III, called "The Great," 223-187) **shall be stirred up, and shall assemble a multitude of great forces:** (Seleucus III raised a great army to invade Egypt, but was assassinated before he could carry out the project) **and one** (Antiochus III) **shall certainly come, and overflow, and pass through** (in 219 B.C., Antiochus III invaded Palestine/Egypt)**: then shall he** (Antiochus III) **return, and be stirred up, even to his** (Antiochus III's) **fortress** (Antiochus III was able to retake Antioch, a capital city in Syria).

11. **And the king of the south** (Ptolemy IV Epiphanes) **shall be moved with choler** (anger)**, and shall come forth and fight with him** (Antiochus III)**, even with the king of the north: and he** (Antiochus III) **shall set forth a great multitude** (Antiochus III invaded Egypt with 70,000 foot soldiers, 6,000 cavalry, and 102 elephants in 217 B.C.)**; but the multitude shall be given into his** (Ptolemy IV's) **hand** (Antiochus III was defeated at the battle of Raphia).

12. **And when he** (Ptolemy IV) **hath taken away the multitude, his** (Ptolemy IV's) **heart shall be lifted up** (Ptolemy tried to offer sacrifices in the Jewish temple precincts, and when he insisted on entering the Holy of Holies, he fell speechless and was dragged out half-dead; he returned to Egypt in a rage)**: and he** (Ptolemy IV) **shall cast down many ten thousands** (disgraced and furious, Ptolemy IV took revenge on the Jews living in Alexandria, Egypt, killing over forty thousand)**: but he** (Ptolemy IV) **shall not be strengthened by it.**

13. **For the king of the north** (Antiochus III) **shall return, and shall set forth a multitude greater than the former, and shall certainly come after certain years** (Antiochus III returned sixteen years later, in 201 B.C., and invaded Egypt) **with a great army and with much riches.**

14. **And in those times there shall many** (Antiochus III of Syria, Philip of Macedonia, and Hannibal of Carthage) **stand up against the king of the south** (the boy-king, Ptolemy V, who was now under the guardianship of the Roman Senate): **also the robbers** (the Romans) **of thy people** (the Jews) **shall exalt themselves** (the Romans) **to establish the vision** (see Daniel 9:24: The Jews could have sealed up the vision concerning the history of pagan Rome after the first advent and the history of papal Rome, by accepting Christ as their Messiah); **but they shall fall** (the prophecy looks far into the future when Rome was eventually divided up by the barbarian invasions of the fifth century).

15. **So the king of the north** (Antiochus III) **shall come, and cast up a mount, and take the most fenced cities** (the Roman general Scopas was besieged in Sidon and forced to surrender; Antiochus then moved south and took the stronghold of Gaza): **and the arms of the south** (Egypt) **shall not withstand, neither his** (Ptolemy IV's) **chosen people** (remember that Antiochus IV chose the Senate of Rome to be the guardians of the boy-king, Ptolemy V), **neither shall there be any strength to withstand** (the Romans, chosen by Ptolemy IV as guardians for the infant king Ptolemy V, were unable to protect Egypt from Antiochus III, who defeated the Roman general Scopas and his 6,000 Greek auxiliaries in 200/199 B.C. Egypt lost many provinces to Philip of Macedon and Antiochus of Syria).

16. **But he** (Rome) **that cometh against him** (Antiochus III specifically, and the Syrian kingdom of the north in general) **shall do according to his** (Rome's) **own will** (Rome defeated Antiochus III in 192 B.C. in Macedonia, and again in 190 B.C. in Asia Minor; in the peace treaty of 188 B.C., Antiochus was forced to give back all of the conquered territories to Egypt. In 168 B.C. Rome compelled Antiochus IV to turn back from invading Egypt. On his way to Syria, Antiochus IV pillaged Jerusalem and the temple, persecuting the Jews and forcing them to stop worshiping God. The Jews revolted in 165 B.C. and

by 164 B.C. had defeated all of the Syrian troops sent against them. In 164 B.C., Antiochus IV died when traveling from the east to Jerusalem to exterminate the Jews. In 63 B.C., Rome conquered the Syrian kingdom of the north), **and none shall stand against him** (Rome. Earlier, in 197 B.C., Rome defeated Philip of Macedon and forced him to return all of the conquered territories to Egypt. In 168 B.C., Rome conquered Macedonia and became master of the Greco-Roman world. Rome also tracked down the last member, Hannibal, of the triple alliance against Egypt, forcing Hannibal to take poison to avoid falling into their hands)**: and he** (Rome) **shall stand in the glorious land** (Jerusalem. Rome in the person of Pompey the Great conquered Palestine in 63 B.C., making Judea a province of Rome), **which by his** (Rome's) **hand shall be consumed** (looking ahead, Gabriel mentions that Rome would in the future destroy the city and temple of Jerusalem in A.D. 70 and, in A.D. 135, demolish Jerusalem for a second time and scatter the Jews throughout the world).

17. **He** (Rome generally, and Julius Caesar specifically, who followed Pompey the Great as the ruler of Rome) **shall also set his** (Julius Caesar's) **face to enter with the strength of his** (Julius Caesar's) **whole kingdom, and upright ones** (Jews who helped Julius Caesar conquer Egypt) **with him** (Julius Caesar)**; thus shall he** (Julius Caesar) **do: and he** (Julius Caesar) **shall give him** (Julius Caesar) **the daughter of women** (Cleopatra. Julius Caesar took 18-year-old Cleopatra, princess of Egypt, as his concubine), **corrupting her** (Cleopatra)**: but she** (Cleopatra) **shall not stand on his** (Rome's generally, and Julius Caesar's specifically) **side, neither be for him** (Rome generally, and specifically Julius Caesar; Cleopatra flirted with Julius Caesar and then with Mark Anthony in order to retain the independence of Egypt and did not act in the interest of Rome).

18. **After this shall he** (Julius Caesar) **turn his** (Julius Caesar's) **face unto the isles, and shall take many** (Caesar conquered the Mediterranean Islands and Africa after Egypt)**: but a prince** (Roman Senator Brutus, who was brought up by Caesar) **for his** (Brutus') **own behalf shall cause the reproach** (Caesar desired to make himself king in fact, if not in name) **offered by him** (Julius Caesar) **to cease; without his** (Julius Caesar's) **own reproach he** (Brutus) **shall cause it to turn upon him** (Julius Caesar. Brutus plotted with sixty senators to assassinate Caesar).

19. **Then he** (Julius Caesar) **shall turn his** (Julius Caesar's) **face toward the fort** (Rome) **of his** (Julius Caesar's) **own land: but he** (Julius Caesar) **shall stumble and fall, and not be found** (Caesar was assassinated in 44 B.C. in the Forum).

20. **Then shall stand up in his** (Julius Caesar's) **estate a raiser of taxes** (Octavius Caesar Augustus, Julius Caesar's nephew, issued the decree in 4 B.C. to tax the world, and this brought Joseph and Mary to Bethlehem—Luke 2:1) **in the glory of the kingdom** (The Pax Romana, beginning with Octavius, lasted a hundred years): **but within few days he** (Octavius Caesar Augustus) **shall be destroyed, neither in anger, nor in battle** (his wife, Livia, had him suffocated after he revived on his deathbed; she did this in order to proclaim Tiberius, whom Octavius despised, the next emperor).

21. **And in his** (Octavius') **estate shall stand up a vile person** (Tiberius, A.D. 14. When Livia asked Octavius to make Tiberius his heir, Octavius said, "Your son is too *vile* to wear the purple of Rome," using the very words of Gabriel to describe the next emperor), **to whom they** (Octavius and the Senate) **shall not give the honor of the kingdom: but he** (Tiberius) **shall come in peaceably, and obtain the kingdom by flatteries.** (Tiberius was a skilled commander of the armies but had a vicious temper and immoral propensities. He was only feared, not liked. He flattered the senators and made promises in order to ascend the throne, but once in power, became a butcher and vile dictator, killing alike those who fawned over him or rejected his vile sexual approaches, often to get hold of their vast estates.)

22. **And with the arms of a flood** (by severe military means, Tiberius put down rebellions against his rule and executed those who plotted to overthrow him) **shall they** (the political enemies of Tiberius) **be overthrown from before him** (Tiberius, who overthrew those that plotted against him), **and shall be broken; yea, also the prince of the covenant** (Jesus Christ, the Prince of the covenant, was crucified in A.D. 31 while Tiberius was still emperor. It was no coincidence that the injustice of Pontius Pilate reflected the injustices perpetrated in the reign of Tiberius).

23. **And after the league** (in 161 B.C., Rome and the Jewish Maccabean leaders made a league of assistance, permitting

Rome to protect them against the Syrian kings and to guarantee their independence) **made with him** (Rome) **he** (Rome) **shall work deceitfully** (in 63 B.C., Pompey disregarded the terms of the league, conquered Judea, and reduced it to a Roman province): **for he** (Rome) **shall come up, and shall become strong with a small people** (incredibly, the small city of Rome ruled the world for over 500 years).

24. **He** (Rome) **shall enter peaceably even upon the fattest places of the province** (Rome gained many of its provinces through legacies or treaties); **and he** (Rome) **shall do that which his** (Rome's) **fathers have not done, nor his** (Rome's) **father's fathers; he** (Rome) **shall scatter among them** (Rome's allies and soldiers) **the prey, and spoil, and riches: yea, and he** (Rome) **shall forecast his** (Rome's) **devices against the strong holds** (the forts and capitals of other nations), **even for a time** (this is prophetic time; the city of Rome would dominate the world for 360 years. This time period would begin at the overthrow of Egypt in 31 B.C., at the battle of Actium, and end in A.D. 330).

25. **And he** (Octavian) **shall stir up his** (Octavian's) **power and his** (Octavian's) **courage against the king of the south** (Mark Antony. Julius Caesar, in 48 B.C., subdued Egypt but did not reduce it to a provincial status. Verses 25-28 now discuss the war between Octavius and Mark Anthony, which resulted in the conquest of Egypt) **with a great army; and the king of the south** (Mark Antony) **shall be stirred up to battle with a very great and mighty army; but he** (Mark Anthony) **shall not stand: for they** (the enemies of Mark Anthony) **shall forecast devices against him** (Mark Anthony).

26. **Yea, they** (Cleopatra and Mark Anthony's intimate friends) **that feed of the portion of his** (Mark Anthony's) **meat shall destroy him** (Mark Anthony committed suicide after Cleopatra and his friends deserted him), **and his** (Octavius') **army shall overflow: and many shall fall down slain** (Octavius defeated Mark Anthony at the great sea and land battle at Actium, 31 B.C.).

27. **And both these kings' hearts** (Octavius' and Mark Anthony's) **shall be to do mischief, and they** (Octavius and Mark Anthony) **shall speak lies at one table; but it shall not prosper: for yet the end shall be at the appointed time** (the appointed time is the end of the 360-year reign of the city of

Rome: from 31 B.C. to A.D. 330. Constantine abandoned the city of Rome in A.D. 330 and moved the capital of the empire to Constantinople).

28. **Then shall he** (Octavius) **return into his** (Octavius') **land** (Rome, Italy) **with great riches** (from Egypt)**; and his** (Rome's) **heart shall be against the holy covenant** (the gospel and God's people. Under Rome, Christ was crucified; Rome also destroyed Jerusalem and its temple in A.D. 70 and persecuted the Christians until A.D. 313)**; and he** (the emperors of Rome) **shall do exploits** (in the hundred years following the reign of Octavius, the Roman Empire reached its farthest expansion and strength)**, and return to his** (Roman emperor's) **own land.**

29. **At the time appointed** (A.D. 330) **he** (Rome) **shall return, and come toward the south** (Egypt and Palestine. Between 284 and 303, Diocletian fought a series of wars to regain and retain Egypt as a Roman province)**; but it shall not be as the former** (B.C. 31)**, or as the latter** (the time of the end, 1798; see verses 40 to 45).

30. **For the ships of Chittim** (Germanic barbarian invaders of the fourth century) **shall come against him** (Valens, AD 378)**: therefore he** (Theodosius A.D. 379 and later Clovis A.D. 508; "It was the Franks alone of all the German tribes who became a wide power in the general history of the middle ages. It is to them that the political inheritance of the Roman Empire passed, to them came the honor of taking up and carrying on, roughly, to be sure, and far less extensively and effectively, but nevertheless of actually carrying on the political work which Rome had been doing." George Burton Adams, *Civilization During the Middle Ages*, (New York: Charles Scribner's Sons, 1900), p. 137.) **shall be grieved, and return, and have indignation against the holy covenant: so shall he** (Rome) **do; he** (Rome generally; specifically Constantine) **shall return, and have intelligence with them** (the bishops) **that forsake the holy covenant.**

31. **And arms** (military support) **shall stand on his** (Clovis') **part** (against the Arian Visigoths, A.D. 507–508)**, and they shall pollute the sanctuary of strength, and shall take away the daily [sacrifice], and shall place the abomination that makes desolate** (in A.D. 508 Clovis united the state with the

church, called here an "abomination" and it would prove to be "desolating" to God's true church for the next 1,290 years; from A.D. 508 until 1798 at which time France separated the church from the state).

32. **And such** (the pontiffs) **as do wickedly against the covenant shall he** (Pepin, Charlemagne, and their successors) **corrupt by flatteries: but the people** (faithful Christians) **that do know their God shall be strong and do exploits** (the courageous stand of the saints for the truth, despite intense persecution, as well as their incisive preaching against the rising tide of evil in the church).

33. **And they** (faithful Christians through the ages) **that understand among the people** (the Christians of Europe) **shall instruct many: yet they** (faithful Christians) **shall fall by the sword, and by flame, by captivity, and by spoil, many days** (the bishops of Rome persecuted the faithful Christians for 1,260 years, the same period of time as the little horn of Daniel 7:25).

34. **Now when they** (faithful Christians) **shall fall, they** (faithful Christians) **shall be holpen with a little help** (the Alpine wilderness, the Great Reformation, and the New World of America provided a refuge for the saints)**: but many** (the scholars of the Renaissance and fickle Christians) **shall cleave to them** (faithful Christians) **with flatteries** (prominent Christians, like Erasmus, were offered emoluments to defect from the truth).

35. **And some of them of understanding** (the reformers and faithful Christians) **shall fall, to try them** (faithful Christians), **and to purge, and to make them white, even to the time of the end** (1798): **because it is yet for a time appointed** (the length of papal reign was predetermined to be a "time, times and half of a time" or 1,260 years, after which it would be punished; see Daniel 7:25).

36. **And the king** (Louis XIV) **shall do according to his will** ("Louis had never been taught gratitude to man or God. Born king, he was taught his importance to the welfare of the State. When Mazarine was dead he felt himself delivered from all obstructions to his will; and, declaring he would govern

according to his own wishes, he took the position which he maintained through life—'I am the State.' " William Henry Foote, D.D., The Huguenots; or, Reformed French Church Harrisonburg, VA: Sprinkle Publications, 2002, pp. 337, 338.); **and he shall exalt himself, and magnify himself above every god, and shall speak marvelous things against the God of gods, and shall prosper until the indignation be accomplished: for that that is determined shall be done** (the eradication of Protestantism from France under Louis XIV resulted in the conditions that bred the Reign of Terror).

37. **Neither shall he** (Revolutionary France) **regard the God of his fathers** (Revolutionary France turned away from European Christianity), **nor the desire of women** (easy divorce was introduced by France and the family was undermined), **nor regard any god: for he** (Revolutionary France) **shall magnify himself** (Revolutionary France) **above all** (the state is god in atheistic political theory).

38. **But in his** (Revolutionary France's) **estate** (realm) **shall he** (Revolutionary France) **honor the God of forces** (evolutionary atheism, the basis of the socialism and communism of today, was exalted into a state religion by Revolutionary France; men now worshiped the forces of nature and not the God of nature): **and a god whom his fathers knew not shall he** (Revolutionary France) **honor with gold, and silver, and with precious stones, and pleasant things.**

39. **Thus shall he** (Revolutionary France) **do in the most strong holds with a strange god** (Revolutionary France exported its neopaganism to Europe by sword and influence), **whom he** (Revolutionary France) **shall acknowledge and increase with glory; and he** (Napoleon Bonaparte) **shall cause them to rule over many** (Napoleon began the conquest of nations in 1797), **and shall divide the land for gain** (before 1798, France confiscated large land holdings and sold them to raise money for the Revolution. Napoleon was at this time a military leader who would have helped empower the government to make this land grab. To quickly facilitate this dividing the land for gain, France issued Assignats).

40. **And at the time of the end** (1798. In Daniel 11:35 and 12:7-9, the phrase *the time of the end* is equated with the end of

the "time, times, and half a time") **shall the king of the south** (south still representing Egypt, as identified in Daniel 11:5-15. The leadership of Egypt was Ibrahim Bey and Murad Bey— Egyptian Mameluke rulers—see Appendix D, page 127) **push at him** (Napoleon Bonaparte. Egypt pushed against the invasion of France in 1798.)**: and the king of the north** (Caliph Selim III of Turkey, the territory of the king of the north; see Daniel 11:5-15) **shall come against him** (Napoleon Bonaparte. Turkey declared war on France in 1798) **like a whirlwind, with chariots, and with horsemen, and with many ships** (Lord Nelson's fleet of ships supported Turkey in its war with France)**; and he** (king of the north—Caliph Selim III of Turkey) **shall enter into the countries, and shall overflow and pass over** (the phrase *overflow and pass over* tells us who prevailed in this battle just described. History records that the Turks prevailed; thus we can be certain that the identity of the pronoun *he* in this sentence is the king of the north. This lets us know that the remaining pronouns in this chapter all refer to the king of the north).

41. **He** (Caliph Selim III of Turkey) **shall enter also into the glorious land,** (Palestine) **and many countries** (*countries* is a supplied word and thus is not in the original) **shall be overthrown** (the Turks reclaimed the territory of Palestine, which Napoleon had just taken)**: but these shall escape out of his** (Caliph Selim III of Turkey) **hand, even Edom, and Moab, and the chief of the children of Ammon** (Edom, Moab, and Ammon, the territory of Jordan, lying outside the limits of Palestine, south and east of the Dead Sea and the Jordan, were out of the line of march of the Turks from Syria to Egypt, so escaped the ravages of that campaign).

42. **He** (Caliph Selim III of Turkey) **shall stretch forth his hand also upon the countries: and the land of Egypt shall not escape** (Egypt once more came under the control of the Turks).

43. **But he** (Caliph Selim III of Turkey) **shall have power over the treasures of gold and of silver, and over all the precious things of Egypt** (Egyptians paid annually to the Turkish government a certain amount of gold and silver, and 600,000 measures of corn and 400,000 of barley)**: and the Libyans and the Ethiopians shall be at his steps** (the unconquered Arabs, who sought the friendship of the Turks and were tributary to them at that time).

44. **But tidings** (intelligence reports) **out of the east** (Persia) **and out of the north** (Russia) **shall trouble him** (Caliph Abdülmecid I of Turkey): **therefore he** (Caliph Abdülmecid I of Turkey) **shall go forth with great fury to destroy, and utterly to make away many** (fulfilled by the Crimean War of 1853-1856, in which Russia and Persia conspired together to destroy the Ottoman Empire but failed in their attempt).

45. **And he** (the king of the north—the leader of Turkey) **shall plant** (place or establish) **the tabernacles of his palace** (a religious/political entity—Islamic Caliphate) **between the seas** (Mediterranean and Dead Seas) **in the glorious holy mountain** (Jerusalem—Mount of Olives); **yet he** (the king of the north) **shall come to his end, and none shall help him** (something will happen that brings the rule of the king of the north to an end. Only verse 45 of this chapter has yet to be fulfilled).

Chapter 12:

1. **And at that time** (immediately following the fulfillment of verse 45) **shall Michael** (Christ; see Appendix F, page 139) **stand up, the great prince which standeth for the children of thy people** (probation closes, Christ puts on His royal robes and reigns): **and there shall be a time of trouble, such as never was since there was a nation even to that same time** (see Revelation 16; Armageddon, the seven last plagues and the destruction of the world at the Second Coming): **and at that time thy people** (all of the saints, not just the Jews) **shall be delivered, everyone that shall be found written in the book.**

Additional historical insights are included in this overview of Daniel 11 from James Henderson's book, *Terror Over Jerusalem*, volume 1 (available at Amazon.com and terroroverjerusalem.com).

Verses 30-45 above are a summary interpretation from the viewpoint of Uriah Smith, which departs from the interpretation that James Henderson provides in his well-researched book.

PRONOUN
IDENTITY

Identifying the Pronoun *He* in Daniel 11:40 As the King of the North

"And at the time of the end shall the king of the south push at him: and the king of the north shall come against him like a whirlwind, with chariots, and with horsemen, and with many ships; *and he shall enter into the countries, and shall overflow and pass over.*"—Daniel 11:40, emphasis supplied.

In the last phrase of Daniel 11:40 we are at a point where the views of the expositors begin to diverge. To whom does the pronoun *he* refer? Who is it that "shall overflow and pass over"? Does the *he* refer to the *him* (France) referred to in this verse, or to the king of the north (Ottoman Empire), or to the king of the south (Egypt)? The identity of the pronouns for the remainder of this chapter depends upon the answer to this question.

On this question two lines of interpretation are maintained. Some (James Henderson, in *Terror Over Jerusalem*) apply the pronoun *he* to the pronoun *him* (France), and endeavor to find a fulfilment in the career of Napoleon. Others apply the pronoun *he* to the king of the north, and accordingly point for a fulfilment to events in the history of Turkey. Some considerations certainly favor the idea that there is, in the latter part of verse 40, a transfer of the burden of the prophecy from the French power to the king of the north. The king of the north is introduced just before, as coming forth like a whirlwind, with chariots, horsemen, and many ships. The collision between this power and the French we have already noticed. The king of the north, with the aid of his allies, gained the day in this contest; and the French, foiled in their efforts, were driven back into Egypt.

Now it would seem to be the more natural application to refer the "overflowing and passing over" to that power which emerged in triumph from that struggle; and that power was Turkey. We will only add that one who is familiar with the Hebrew assures us that the construction of this passage is such as to make it necessary to refer the overflowing and passing over to the king of the north, these words expressing the result of that movement which is just before likened to the fury of the whirlwind.[1]

All the major battles predicted in chapter 11 report the outcome. The prophecy foretells which side wins. In verse 10 it says: "But his sons shall be stirred up, and shall assemble a multitude of great forces: and one shall certainly come, *and overflow, and pass through:* then shall he return, and be stirred up, even to his fortress."

That phrase, *overflow, and pass through* indicates which side won the battle. Note this in verse 10:

> **But his** (Seleucus II's) **sons** (Seleucus III Ceraunus Soter, 225-223, and Antiochus III, called "The Great," 223-187) **shall be stirred up, and assemble a multitude of great forces:** (Seleucus III raised a great army to invade Egypt, but was assassinated before he could carry out the project) **and one** (Antiochus III) **shall certainly come, and *overflow, and pass through*** (in 219 B.C., Antiochus III invaded Palestine/Egypt): **then shall he** (Antiochus III) **return and be stirred up, even to his** (Antiochus III 's) **fortress** (Antiochus III was able to retake Antioch, a capital city in Syria).

We see the word *overflow* also in verse 26: "Yea, they that feed of the portion of his meat shall destroy him, and his army shall *overflow:* and many shall fall down slain." The army that overflowed won:

> **Yea, they** (Cleopatra and Mark Anthony's intimate friends) **that feed of the portion of his** (Mark Anthony's) **meat shall destroy him** (Mark Anthony committed suicide after Cleopatra and his friends deserted him)**, and his** (Octavius') **army shall *overflow:* and many shall fall down slain** (Octavius defeated Mark Anthony at the great sea and land battle at Actium, 31 B.C.).

Now, when we get to verse 40, if we separate the last part of the sentence from the first part, we would not be told who won the battle. Verse 40 is all one sentence. The last clause says, "and he shall enter into the countries, and *shall overflow and pass over.*" It makes sense to keep the entire sentence all referring to one battle in one area of the world.

---

1. Paraphrased from Uriah Smith, *Daniel and the Revelation* (1912), 305, 306.

Without that last part of the sentence we are not told if the *him* wins or if the king of the north wins or if the king of the south wins. All we know is that the king of the south pushes *him*. Does that push indicate a victory over the *him*? We are not told. Next we are told that the king of the north comes against him "like a whirlwind, with chariots, and with horsemen, and with many ships . . ." We are not told if the *him* who refers to Napoleon, as identified by the previous verse, wins or is defeated in this encounter. This would be very unusual, because all of the major battles predicted in chapter 11 tell us who the winner is. When we look into the historical record we see that the king of the north (Ottoman Empire) with his alliance of ships defeats the *him* (Napoleon). France left that part of the world without gaining their objective. The king of the north won that contest. Thus the phrase *overflowed and passed over* which denotes victory applies to the king of the north.

I think there is very strong evidence that the *he* in the last clause of the sentence refers to the king of the north rather than to France. I think that it is compelling to see the use of the word *overflow* being used three times and each time indicating who the winner of the just mentioned battle is. Therefore, it can be concluded that the rest of the pronouns in verses 41-45 will be referring to the king of the north. There is no question that the *he* in Daniel 11:45 is referring to none other than the leader of present-day Turkey.

THE FRENCH REVOLUTION

Is France the king spoken of in Daniel 11:36, thus making France the identity for the pronoun *him* found in Daniel 11:40?[1]

"VERSE 36. And the king shall do according to his will; and he shall exalt himself, and magnify himself above every god, and shall speak marvelous things against the God of gods, and shall prosper till the indignation be accomplished; for that that is determined shall be done."

The king here introduced cannot denote the same power which was last noticed; namely, the papal power; for the specifications will not hold good if applied to that power.

Take a declaration in the next verse: "Nor regard any god." This has never been true of the papacy. God and Christ, though often placed in a false position, have never been professedly set aside and rejected from that system of religion. The only difficulty in applying it to a new power lies in the definite article the; for, it is urged, the expression "the king" would identify this as one last spoken of. If it could be properly translated a king, there would be no difficulty; and it is said that some of the best Biblical critics give it this rendering, Mede, Wintle, Boothroyd, and others translating the passage, "A certain king shall do according to his will," thus clearly introducing a new power upon the stage of action.

Three peculiar features must appear in the power which fulfills this

---

1. This Appendix section is from Uriah Smith, *Daniel and the Revelation*, 292-302.

prophecy: (1) It must assume the character here delineated near the commencement of the time of the end, to which we were brought down in the preceding verse; (2) it must be a willful power; (3) it must be an atheistical power; or perhaps the two latter specifications might be united by saying that its willfulness would be manifested in the direction of atheism. A revolution exactly answering to this description did take place in France at the time indicated in the prophecy. Voltaire had sowed the seeds which bore their legitimate and baleful fruit. That boastful infidel, in his pompous but impotent self-conceit, had said, "I am weary of hearing people repeat that twelve men established the Christian religion. I will prove that one man may suffice to overthrow it." Associating with himself such men as Rousseau, D'Alembert, Diderot, and others, he undertook the work. They sowed to the wind, and reaped the whirlwind. Their efforts culminated in the "reign of terror" of 1793, when the Bible was discarded, and the existence of the Deity denied, as the voice of the nation.

The historian thus describes this great religious change:

"It was not enough, they said, for a regenerate nation to have dethroned earthly kings, unless she stretched out the arm of defiance toward those powers which superstition had represented as reigning over boundless space."—Scott's *Napoleon*, Vol. I, p.172.

Again he says:

"The constitutional bishop of Paris was brought forward to play the principal part in the most impudent and scandalous farce ever enacted in the face of a national representation . . . He was brought forward in full procession, to declare to the convention that the religion which he had taught so many years was, in every respect a piece of PRIESTCRAFT, which had no foundation either in history or sacred truth. He disowned, in solemn and explicit terms, the EXISTENCE OF THE DEITY, to whose worship he had been consecrated, and devoted himself in future to the homage of Liberty, Equality, Virtue and Morality. He then laid on the table his episcopal decoration, and received a fraternal embrace from the president of the convention. Several apostate priests followed the example of this prelate. . . . The world, for the FIRST time heard an assembly of men, born and educated in civilization, and assuming the right to govern one of the finest of the European nations, uplift their united voice to DENY the most solemn truth which man's soul receives, and RENOUNCE UNANIMOUSLY THE BELIEF AND WORSHIP OF DEITY." - Id., Vol. I, p. 173.

A writer in *Blackwood's Magazine,* November, 1870, said:

"France is the only nation in the world concerning which the authentic record survives, that as a nation she lifted her hand in open rebellion against the Author of the universe. Plenty of blasphemers, plenty of infidels, there have been, and still continue to be, in England, Germany, Spain, and elsewhere; but France stands apart in the world's history as the single state which, by the decree of her legislative assembly, pronounced that there was no God, and of which the entire population of the capital, and a vast majority elsewhere, women as well as men, danced and sang with joy in accepting the announcement."

But there are other and still more striking specifications which were fulfilled in this power.

"VERSE 37. Neither shall he regard the God of his fathers, nor the desire of women, nor regard any god: for he shall magnify himself above all."

The Hebrew word for woman is also translated wife; and Bishop Newton observes that this passage would be more properly rendered "the desire of wives." This would seem to indicate that this government, at the same time it declared that God did not exist, would trample underfoot the law which God had given to regulate the marriage institution. And we find that the historian has, unconsciously perhaps, and if so all the more significantly, coupled together the atheism and licentiousness of this government in the same order in which they are presented in the prophecy. He says:

"Intimately connected with these laws affecting religion was that which reduced the union of marriage—the most sacred engagements which human beings can form, and the permanence of which leads most strongly to the consolidation of society—to the state of a mere civil contract of a transitory character, which any two persons might engage in and cast loose at pleasure, when their taste was changed or their appetite gratified. If fiends had set themselves at work to discover a mode most effectually destroying whatever is venerable, graceful, or permanent in domestic life, and obtaining at the same time an assurance that the mischief which it was their object to create should be perpetuated from one generation to another, they could not have invented a more effectual plan than the degradation of marriage into a state of mere occasional cohabitation or licensed concubinage. Sophie Arnoult, an actress famous for the witty things she said, described the republican marriage as the sacrament of adultery. These anti-religious and anti-social regulations

121

did not answer the purpose of the frantic and inconsiderate zealots by whom they had been urged forward."—Scott's *Napoleon*, Vol. I, p.173.

"Nor regard any god." In addition to the testimony already presented to show the utter atheism of the nation at this time, the following fearful language of madness and presumption is to be recorded:

"The fear of God is so far from being the beginning of wisdom that it is the beginning of folly. Modesty is only the invention of refined voluptuousness. The Supreme King, the God of the Jews and the Christians, is but a phantom. Jesus Christ is an impostor."

Another writer says:

"Aug. 26, 1792, an open confession of atheism was made by the National Convention; and corresponding societies and atheistical clubs were everywhere fearlessly held in the French nation. Massacres and the reign of terror became the most horrid."—Smith's *Key to Revelation*, p.323.

"Hebert, Chaumette, and their associates appeared at the bar, and declared that God did not exist."—Alison, Vol. I, p.150.

At this juncture all religious worship was prohibited except that of liberty and the country. The gold and silver plate of the churches was seized upon and desecrated. The churches were closed. The bells were broken and cast into cannon. The Bible was publicly burned. The sacramental vessels were paraded through the streets on an ass, in token of contempt. A week of ten days instead of seven was established, and death was declared, in conspicuous letters posted over their burial places, to be an eternal sleep. But the crowning blasphemy, if these orgies of hell admit of degrees, remained to be performed by the comedian Monvel, who, as a priest of Illuminism, said:

"God, if you exist, avenge your injured name. I bid you defiance! You remain silent. You dare not launch your thunders! Who, after this, will believe in your existence? The whole ecclesiastical establishment was destroyed."—Scott's *Napoleon*, Vol. I, p.173.

Behold what man is when left to himself, and what infidelity is when the restraints of law are thrown off, and it has the power in its own hands! Can it be doubted that these scenes are what the omniscient One foresaw, and noted on the sacred page, when he pointed out a kingdom to arise which should exalt itself above every god, and disregard them all?

"VERSE 38. But in his estate shall he honor the God of forces:

and a god whom his fathers knew not shall he honor with gold, and silver, and with precious stones, and pleasant things."

We meet a seeming contradiction in this verse. How can a nation disregard every god, and yet honor the god of forces? It could not at one and the same time hold both these positions; but it might for a time disregard all gods, and then subsequently introduce another worship and regard the god of forces. Did such a change occur in France at this time?—It did. The attempt to make France a godless nation produced such anarchy that the rulers feared the power would pass entirely out of their hands, and therefore perceived that, as a political necessity, some kind of worship must be introduced; but they did not intend to introduce any movement which would increase devotion, or develop any true spiritual character among the people, but only such as would keep themselves in power, and give them control of the national forces. A few extracts from history will show this. Liberty and country were at first the objects of adoration. "Liberty, equality, virtue, and morality," the very opposites of anything they possessed in fact or exhibited in practice, were words which they set forth as describing the deity of the nation. In 1793 the worship of the Goddess of Reason was introduced, and is thus described by the historian:

"One of the ceremonies of this insane time stands unrivaled for absurdity combined with impiety. The doors of the convention were thrown open to a band of musicians, preceded by whom, the members of the municipal body entered in solemn procession, singing a hymn in praise of liberty, and escorting, as the object of their future worship, a veiled female whom they termed the Goddess of Reason. Being brought within the bar, she was unveiled with great form, and placed on the right hand of the president, when she was generally recognized as a dancing girl of the opera, with whose charms most of the persons present were acquainted from her appearance on the stage, while the experience of individuals was further extended. To this person, as the fittest representative of that reason whom they worshiped, the National Convention of France rendered public homage. This impious and ridiculous mummery had a certain fashion; and the installation of the Goddess of Reason was renewed and imitated throughout the nation, in such places where the inhabitants desired to show themselves equal to all the heights of the Revolution."—Scott's *Napoleon*, Vol. 1, Ch.17.

In introducing the worship of Reason, in 1794, Chaumette said:

"'Legislative fanaticism has lost its hold; it has given place to reason. We have left its temples; they are regenerated. Today an immense multitude are assembled under its Gothic roofs, which, for the first time, will re-echo the voice of truth. There the French will celebrate their true worship—that of Liberty and Reason. There we will form new vows for the prosperity of the armies of the Republic; there we will abandon the worship of inanimate idols for that of Reason—this animated image, the masterpiece of creation."

"A veiled female, arrayed in blue drapery, was brought into the convention; and Chaumette, taking her by the hand,

"'Mortals,' said he, 'cease to tremble before the powerless thunders of a God whom your fears have created. Henceforth acknowledge NO DIVINITY but REASON. I offer you its noblest and purest image; if you must have idols, sacrifice only to such as this. . . . Fall before the august Senate of Freedom, Vail of Reason.'

"At the same time the goddess appeared, personified by a celebrated beauty, Madame Millard, of the opera, known in more than one character to most of the convention. The goddess, after being embraced by the president, was mounted on a magnificent car, and conducted, amidst an immense crowd, to the cathedral of Notre Dame, to take the place of the Deity. There she was elevated on the high altar, and received the adoration of all present.

"On the 11th of November, the popular society of the museum entered the hall of the municipality, exclaiming, 'Vive la Raison!' and carrying on the top of a pole the half-burned remains of several books, among others the breviaries and the Old and New Testaments, which 'expiated in a great fire,' said the president, 'all the fooleries which they have made the human race commit.'

"The most sacred relations of life were at the same period placed on a new footing suited to the extravagant ideas of the times. Marriage was declared a civil contract, binding only during the pleasure of the contracting parties. Mademoiselle Arnoult, a celebrated comedian, expressed the public feeling when she called 'marriage the sacrament of adultery.'"—Id.

Truly this was a strange god, whom the fathers of that generation knew not. No such deity had ever before been set up as an object of adoration. And well might it be called the god of forces; for the object of the movement was to cause the people to renew their covenant and repeat their vows for the prosperity of the armies of France. Read again a few lines from the extract already given:

"We have left its temples; they are regenerated. Today an immense multitude is assembled under its Gothic roofs, which for the first time, will re-echo the voice of truth. There the French will celebrate their true worship,—that of Liberty and Reason. There we will form new vows for the prosperity of the armies of the Republic."

During the time while the fantastic worship of reason was the national craze, the leaders of the revolution are known to history as "the atheists." But it was soon perceived that a religion with more powerful sanctions than the one then in vogue must be instituted to hold the people. A form of worship therefore followed in which the object of adoration was the "Supreme Being." It was equally hollow so far as any reformation of life and vital godliness were concerned, but it took hold upon the supernatural. And while the Goddess of Reason was indeed a "strange god," the statement in regard to honoring the "God of forces," may perhaps more appropriately be referred to this latter phase. See Thier's "French Revolution."

"VERSE 39. Thus shall he do in the most strong holds with a strange god, whom he shall acknowledge and increase with glory: and he shall cause them to rule over many, and shall divide the land for gain."

The system of paganism which had been introduced into France, as exemplified in the worship of the idol set up in the person of the Goddess of Reason, and regulated by a heathen ritual which had been enacted by the National Assembly for the use of the French people, continued in force till the appointment of Napoleon to the provisional consulate of France in 1799. The adherents of this strange religion occupied the fortified places, the strongholds of the nation, as expressed in this verse.

But that which serves to identify the application of this prophecy to France, perhaps as clearly as any other particular, is the statement made in the last clause of the verse; namely, that they should "divide the land for gain." Previous to the Revolution, the landed property of France was owned by a few landlords in immense estates. These estates were required by the law to remain undivided, so that no heirs or creditors could partition them. But revolution knows no law; and in the anarchy that now reigned, as noted also in the eleventh of Revelation, the titles of the nobility were abolished, and their lands disposed of in small parcels for the benefit of the public exchequer. The government was in need of funds, and these large landed estates were confiscated, and sold at auction in parcels to suit purchasers. The historian thus records this unique transaction:

"The confiscation of two thirds of the landed property of the kingdom, which arose from the decrees of the convention against the emigrants, clergy, and persons convicted at the Revolutionary Tribunals, . . . placed funds worth above L700,000,000 sterling at the disposal of the government."—Alison, Vol. IV, p.151.

When did ever an event transpire, and in what country, fulfilling a prophecy more completely than this? As the nation began to come to itself, a more rational religion was demanded, and the heathen ritual was abolished. The historian thus describes that event:

"A third and bolder measure was the discarding of the heathen ritual and re-opening the churches for Christian worship; and of this the credit was wholly Napoleon's, who had to contend with the philosophic prejudices of almost all his colleagues. He, in his conversation with them, made no attempts to represent himself a believer in Christianity, but stood only on the necessity of providing the people with the regular means of worship wherever it is meant to have a state of tranquility. The priests who chose to take the oath of fidelity to the government were readmitted to their functions; and this wise measure was followed by the adherence of not less than 20,000 of these ministers of religion, who had hitherto languished in the prisons of France."—Lockhart's *Life of Napoleon*, Vol. I, p.154.

Thus terminated the Reign of Terror and the Infidel Revolution. Out of the ruins rose Bonaparte, to guide the tumult to his own elevation, place himself at the head of the French government, and strike terror to the hearts of nations.

KING OF THE SOUTH

Who was the King of the South in 1798?

When the battle described in Daniel 11:40 took place (1798), who was the king of the south? Who was in charge of Ptolemy's Egyptian territory? On the following map, we see that the Ottoman Empire obtained control of this southern territory in 1512:

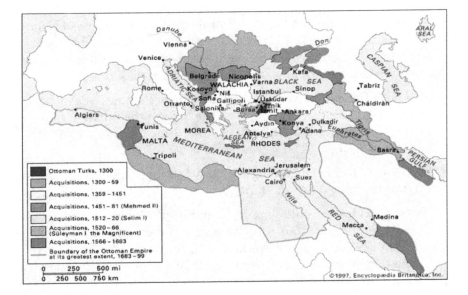

And from this map, we see that it lost this territory in 1879:

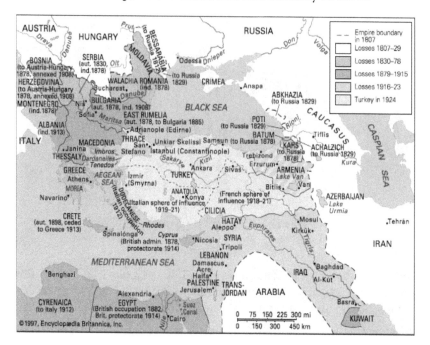

And yet, if the Ottoman Empire controlled Egypt at the time of Napoleon's invasion, then we would have the king of the north pushing against France when they invaded Egypt. But the verse says that it would be the king of the south, not the king of the north that pushes against the "him":

> **"And at the time of the end shall the king of the south** (Egyptian ruler) **push at him** (Napoleon): **and the king of the north** (Caliph Selim III of Turkey) **shall come against him** (Napoleon) **like a whirlwind"**—Daniel 11:40.

If Napoleon had been battling the Ottoman Empire upon landing in Egypt, this history would not fit the verse.

But as providence would have it, Igrahim and Murad—Mamluk rulers—had taken Egypt from the Ottoman Empire and were co-ruling Egypt from 1791 up until the invasion of Napoleon. So the Sultan of the Ottoman Empire was not controlling Egypt; thus he was not the one who pushed against Napoleon when Napoleon invaded Egypt.

I consider it quite amazing that this prophecy fits so well with the actual facts of history. Following is the documentation to support the fact that the Ottoman Empire was not ruling Egypt at the time of Napoleon's invasion:

"In late 1785, Ibrahim and Murad received Ottoman demands for tribute but refused to comply. On 18 July 1786, Murad Bey failed to contain the Ottoman expeditionary force sent against him, as a result of which the Turks set up a new government in Cairo in August 1786. Murad and Ibrahim Bey withdrew to Upper Egypt where they resisted the Ottoman forces for the next six years. Returning to Cairo in July 1791, Murad Bey continued ruling Egypt for seven years, sharing power with Ibrahim Bey. In 1798, he served as sari askar (commander-in-chief) of the Mamluk forces against the French troops under General Napoleon Bonaparte but was decisively defeated at Shubra Khit (10-13 July) and Inbaba (Embaba) (21 July). He rejected Napoleon's offer to govern Girga province and withdrew to Upper Egypt, where he tied down considerable numbers of French troops under General Desaix. Demonstrating notable administrative and military skills, he fought the French to a draw at Sediman (El Lahun, 7 October 1798) but was defeated at Samhud (22 January 1799). Nevertheless, his guerrillas constantly harassed the French communication and supply lines."[1]

"Ottomans attempted to restore control from Murad Bey and Ibrahim Bey but at no avail. Nevertheless, they both failed to defend Egypt against the French invasion led by Napoleon Bonaparte in 1798. A fierce battle took place between the two sides near Imbaba in Cairo. The Mamluks were defeated, while those who survived from the battle defected the country including both Murad Bey and Ibrahim Bey who carried their treasures and hastily left Egypt."[2]

"With time he (Ibrahim Bey) emerged as one of the most influential Mamluk commanders, sharing a de facto control of Egypt with his fellow Georgian Murad Bey."[3]

Let's look at our text again:

"And at the time of the end shall the king of the south push at him: and the king of the north shall come against him like a whirlwind, with chariots, and with horsemen, and with many ships; and he shall enter into the countries, and shall overflow and pass over"—Daniel 11:40.

---

1   <http://tinyurl.com/q2sxwqj>.

2   <http://www.youregypt.com/ehistory/history/islamic/ottomans/>.

3   <http://en.wikipedia.org/wiki/Ibrahim_Bey_(Mamluk)>.

JERUSALEM CALIPHATE AND THE THIRD JIHAD

History tells us that Napoleon headed north from Egypt in 1799 to conquer the Turks. They declared war upon Napoleon and came against him and his army like a whirlwind, ultimately reclaiming their southern territory with the help of English ships. Verses 41 to 43 follow the historical fulfillment of this war between Napoleon and the sultan of Turkey.

TRIANGULAR WARFARE

Uriah Smith's (1912) Interpretation of Daniel 11:40-44[1]

"VERSE 40. And at the time of the end shall the king of the south push at him: and the king of the north shall come against him like a whirlwind, with chariots, and with horsemen, and with many ships: and he shall enter into the countries, and shall overflow and pass over."

After a long interval, the king of the south and the king of the north again appear on the stage of action. We have met with nothing to indicate that we are to look to any localities for these powers other than those which, shortly after the death of Alexander, constituted respectively the southern and northern divisions of his empire. The king of the south was at that time Egypt, and the king of the north was Syria, including Thrace and Asia Minor. Egypt is still, by common agreement, the king of the south, while the territory which at first constituted the king of the north, has been for the past four hundred years wholly included within the dominions of the sultan of Turkey. To Egypt and Turkey, then, in connection with the power last under consideration, we must look for a fulfilment of the verse before us.

This application of the prophecy calls for a conflict to spring up between Egypt and France, and Turkey and France, in 1798, which year, as we have seen, marked the beginning of the time of the end; and if history testifies that such a triangular war did break out in that year, it will be conclusive proof of the correctness of the application.

---

1. Uriah Smith, *Daniel and the Revelation*, 1912, 302-310.

We inquire, therefore, Is it a fact that at the time of the end, Egypt did "push," or make a comparatively feeble resistance, while Turkey did come like a resistless "whirlwind," against "him," that is, the government of France? We have already produced some evidence that the time of the end commenced in 1798; and no reader of history need be informed that in that very year a state of open hostility between France and Egypt was inaugurated.

To what extent this conflict owed its origin to the dreams of glory deliriously cherished in the ambitious brain of Napoleon Bonaparte, the historian will form his own opinion; but the French, or Napoleon at least, contrived to make Egypt the aggressor. Thus, when in the invasion of that country he had secured his first foothold in Alexandria, he declared that "he had not come to ravage the country or to wrest it from the Grand Seignior, but merely to deliver it from the domination of the Mamelukes, and to revenge the outrages which they had committed against France."— Thier's *French Revolution,* Vol. IV, p.268.

Again the historian says: "Besides, he [Bonaparte] had strong reasons to urge against them [the Mamelukes]; for they had never ceased to ill-treat the French."—Id., p.273.

The beginning of the year 1798 found France indulging in immense projects against the English. The Directory desired Bonaparte to undertake at once a descent upon England; but he saw that no direct operations of that kind could be judiciously undertaken before the fall, and he was unwilling to hazard his growing reputation by spending the summer in idleness. "But," says the historian, "he saw a far-off land, where a glory was to be won which would gain a new charm in the eyes of his countrymen by the romance and mystery which hung upon the scene. Egypt, the land of the Pharoahs and the Ptolemies, would be a noble field for new triumphs."—White's *History of France,* p.469.

But while still broader visions of glory opened before the eyes of Bonaparte in those Eastern historic lands, covering not Egypt only, but Syria, Persia, Hindustan, even to the Ganges itself, he had no difficulty in persuading the Directory that Egypt was the vulnerable point through which to strike at England by intercepting her Eastern trade. Hence on the pretext above mentioned, the Egyptian campaign was undertaken.

The downfall of the papacy, which marked the termination of the 1260 years, and according to verse 35 showed the commencement of the time of the end, occurred on the 10th of February, 1798, when Rome fell into the hands of Berthier, the general of the French. On the 5th of March following, Bonaparte received the decree of the Directory relative to the expedition against Egypt. He left Paris May 3, and set sail from Toulon the 29th, with a large naval armament consisting of 500 sail, carrying 40,000 soldiers and 10,000 sailors. July 5, Alexandria was taken, and immediately fortified. On the 23rd the decisive battle of the pyramids was fought, in which the Mamelukes contested the field with valor and desperation, but were no match for the disciplined legions of the French. Murad Bey lost all his cannon, 400 camels, and 3,000 men. The loss of the French was comparatively slight. On the 24th, Bonaparte entered Cairo, the capital of Egypt, and only waited the subsidence of the floods of the Nile to pursue Murad Bey to Upper Egypt, whither he had retired with his shattered cavalry, and so make a conquest of the whole country. Thus the king of the south was able to make a feeble resistance.

At this juncture, however, the situation of Napoleon began to grow precarious. The French fleet, which was his only channel of communication with France, was destroyed by the English under Nelson at Aboukir; and on September 2 of this same year, 1798, the sultan of Turkey, under feelings of jealousy against France, artfully fostered by the English ambassadors at Constantinople, and exasperated that Egypt, so long a semi-dependency of the Ottoman empire, should be transformed into a French province, declared war against France. Thus the king of the north (Turkey) came against him (France) in the same year that the king of the south (Egypt) "pushed," and both "at the time of the end:" which is another conclusive proof that the year 1798 is the year which begins that period; and all of which is a demonstration that this application of the prophecy is correct; for so many events meeting so accurately the specifications of the prophecy could not take place together, and not constitute a fulfilment of the prophecy.

Was the coming of the king of the north, or Turkey, like a whirlwind in comparison with the pushing of Egypt? Napoleon had crushed the armies of Egypt; he assayed to do the same thing with the armies of the sultan, who were menacing an attack from the side of Asia. Feb.27, 1799, with 18,000 men, he commenced his march from Cairo to Syria. He first took the fort of El- Arish, in the desert, then Jaffa (the Joppa of the Bible), conquered the inhabitants of Naplous at Zeta, and was again victorious at Jafet. Meanwhile, a strong body of Turks had intrenched themselves at St. Jean d'Acre, while swarms of Mussulmans gathered in the mountains of Samaria, ready to swoop down upon the French when they should besiege Acre. Sir Sidney Smith at the same time appeared before St. Jean d'Acre with two English ships, reinforced the Turkish garrison of that place, and captured the apparatus for the siege, which Napoleon had sent across by sea from Alexandria. A Turkish fleet soon appeared in the offing, which, with the Russian and English vessels then cooperating with them, constituted the "many ships" of the king of the north.

On the 18th of March the siege commenced. Napoleon was twice called away to save some French divisions from falling into the hands of the Mussulman hordes that filled the country. Twice also a breach was made in the wall of the city; but the assailants were met with such fury by the garrison, that they were obliged, despite their best efforts, to give over the struggle. After a continuance of sixty days, Napoleon raised the siege, sounded, for the first time in his career, the note of retreat, and on the 21st of May, 1799, commenced to retrace his steps to Egypt.

"And he shall overflow and pass over." We have found events which furnish a very striking fulfilment of the pushing of the king of the south, and the whirlwind onset of the king of the north against the French power. Thus far there is quite a general agreement in the application of the prophecy. We now reach a point where the views of the expositors begin to diverge. To whom do the words he "shall overflow and pass over," refer?—to France or to the king of the north? The application of the remainder of this chapter depends upon the answer to this question. From this point two lines of interpretation are maintained. Some apply the words to France, and endeavor to find a fulfilment in the career of Napoleon. Others apply them to the king of the north, and accordingly point for a fulfilment to events in the history of Turkey. We speak of these two positions only, as the attempt which some make to bring in the papacy here is so evidently wide of the mark that its consideration need not detain us. If neither of these positions is free from difficulty, as we presume no one will claim that it is, absolutely, it only remains that we take that one which has the weight of evidence in its favor. And we shall find one in favor of which the evidence does so greatly preponderate, to the exclusion of all others as scarcely to leave any room for doubt in regard to the view here mentioned.

Respecting the application of this portion of the prophecy to Napoleon or to France under his leadership, so far as we are acquainted with his history, we do not find events which we can urge with any degree of assurance as the fulfilment of the remaining portion of this chapter, and hence do not see how it can be thus applied. It must, then, be fulfilled by Turkey, unless it can be shown (1) that the expression "king of the north" does not apply to Turkey, or (2) that there is some other power besides either France or the king of the north which fulfilled this part of the prediction. But if Turkey, now occupying the territory which constituted the northern division of Alexander's empire, is not the king of the north of this prophecy, then we are left without any principle to guide us in the interpretation; and we presume all will agree that there is no room for the introduction of any other power here. The French king, and the king of the north, are the only ones to whom the prediction can apply. The fulfilment must lie between them.

Some considerations certainly favor the idea that there is, in the latter part of verse 40, a transfer of the burden of the prophecy from the French power to the king of the north. The king of the north is introduced just before, as coming forth like a whirlwind, with chariots, horsemen, and many ships. The collision between this power and the French we have already noticed. The king of the north, with the aid of his allies, gained the day in this contest; and the French, foiled in their efforts, were driven back into Egypt. Now it would seem to be the more natural application to refer the "overflowing and passing over" to that power which emerged in triumph from that struggle; and that power was Turkey. We will only add that one who is familiar with the Hebrew assures us that the construction of this passage is such as to make it necessary to refer the overflowing and passing over to the king of the north, these words expressing the result of that movement which is just before likened to the fury of the whirlwind.

"VERSE 41. He shall enter also into the glorious land, and many countries shall be overthrown: but these shall escape out of his hand, even Edom, and Moab, and the chief of the children of Ammon."

The facts just stated relative to the campaign of the French against Turkey, and the repulse of the former at St. Jean d'Acre, were drawn chiefly from the Encyclopedia Americana. From the same source we gather further particulars respecting the retreat of the French into Egypt, and the additional reverses which compelled them to evacuate that country.

Abandoning a campaign in which one third of the army had fallen victims to war and the plague, the French retired from St. Jean d'Acre, and after a fatiguing march of twenty-six days re-entered Cairo in Egypt. They thus abandoned all the conquests they had made in Judea; and the "glorious land," Palestine, with all its provinces, here called "countries," fell back again under the oppressive rule of the Turk. Edom, Moab, and Ammon, lying outside the limits of Palestine, south and east of the Dead Sea and the Jordan, were out of the line of march of the Turks from Syria to Egypt, and so escaped the ravages of that campaign. On this passage, Adam Clarke has the following note: "These and other Arabians, they [the Turks] have never been able to subdue. They still occupy the deserts, and receive a yearly pension of forty thousand crowns of gold from the Ottoman emperors to permit the caravans with the pilgrims for Mecca to have a free passage."

"VERSE 42. He shall stretch forth his hand also upon the countries: and the land of Egypt shall not escape."

On the retreat of the French to Egypt, a Turkish fleet landed 18,000 men at Aboukir. Napoleon immediately attacked the place, completely routing the Turks, and re-establishing his authority in Egypt. But at this point, severe reverses to the French arms in Europe called Napoleon home to look after the interests of his own country. The command of the troops in Egypt was left with General Kleber, who, after a period of untiring activity for the benefit of the army, was murdered by a Turk in Cairo, and the command was left with Abdallah Manou. With an army which could not be recruited, every loss was serious.

Meanwhile, the English government, as the ally of the Turks, had resolved to wrest Egypt from the French. March 13, 1800, an English fleet disembarked a body of troops at Aboukir. The French gave battle the next day, but were forced to retire. On the 18th Aboukir surrendered. On the 28th reinforcements were brought by a Turkish fleet, and the grand vizier approached from Syria with a large army. The 19th, Rosetta surrendered to the combined forces of the English and Turks. At Ramanieh a French corps of 4,000 men was defeated by 8,000 English and 6,000 Turks. At El-menayer 5,000 French were obliged to retreat, May 16, by the vizier, who was pressing forward to Cairo with 20,000 men. The whole French army was now shut up in Cairo and Alexandria. Cairo capitulated June 27, and Alexandria, September 2. Four weeks after, Oct.1, 1801, the preliminaries of peace were signed at London.

"Egypt shall not escape" were the words of the prophecy. This language seems to imply that Egypt would be brought into subjection to some power from whose dominion it would desire to be released. As between the French and Turks, how did this question stand with the Egyptians?—They preferred French rule. In R.R. Madden's Travels in Egypt, Nubia, Turkey, and Palestine in the years 1824-1827, published in London in 1829, it is stated that the French were much regretted by the Egyptians, and extolled as benefactors; that "for the short period they remained, they left traces of amelioration;" and that, if they could have established their power, Egypt would now be comparatively civilized. In view of this testimony, the language would not be appropriate if applied to the French; the Egyptians did not desire to escape out of their hands. They did desire to escape from the hands of the Turks, but could not.

"VERSE 43. But he shall have power over the treasures of gold and of silver, and over all the precious things of Egypt: and the Libyans and the Ethiopians shall be at his steps."

136

In illustration of this verse we quote the following from *Historic Echoes of the Voice of God*, p. 49:

"History gives the following facts: When the French were driven out of Egypt, and the Turks took possession, the sultan permitted the Egyptians to reorganize their government as it was before the French invasion. He asked of the Egyptians neither soldiers, guns, nor fortifications, but left them to manage their own affairs independently, with the important exception of putting the nation under tribute to himself. In the articles of agreement between the sultan and the pasha of Egypt, it was stipulated that the Egyptians should pay annually to the Turkish government a certain amount of gold and silver, and 'six hundred thousand measures of corn, and four hundred thousand of barley.'"

"The Libyans and the Ethiopians," "the Cushim," says Dr. Clarke, "the unconquered Arabs," who have sought the friendship of the Turks, and many of whom are tributary to them at the present time.

"VERSE 44. But tidings out of the east and out of the north shall trouble him: therefore he shall go forth with great fury to destroy, and utterly to make away many."

On this verse Dr. Clarke has a note which is worthy of mention. He says: "This part of the prophecy is allowed to be yet unfulfilled." His note was printed in 1825. In another portion of his comment, he says: "If the Turkish power be understood, as in the preceding verses, it may mean that the Persians on the east, and the Russians on the north, will at some time greatly embarrass the Ottoman government."

Between this conjecture of Dr. Clarke's, written in 1825, and the Crimean War of 1853-1856, there is certainly a striking coincidence, inasmuch as the very powers he mentions, the Persians on the east and the Russians on the north, were the ones which instigated that conflict. Tidings from these powers troubled him (Turkey). Their attitude and movements incited the sultan to anger and revenge. Russia, being the more aggressive party, was the object of attack. Turkey declared war on her powerful northern neighbor in 1853. The world looked on in amazement to see a government which had long been called "the Sick Man of the East," a government whose army was dispirited and demoralized, whose treasuries were empty, whose rulers were vile and imbecile, and whose subjects were rebellious and threatening secession, rush with such impetuosity into the conflict. The prophecy said that they should go forth with "great fury;" and when they thus went forth in the war aforesaid, they were described, in the profane vernacular of an American writer, as "fighting like devils." England and France, it is true, soon came to the help of Turkey; but she went forth in the manner described, and as is reported, gained important victories before receiving the assistance of these powers.

MICHAEL WHO?

The Biblical Evidence Supporting the Fact That Michael Is Another Name for Jesus[1]

The name *Michael* is used five times in the Bible to designate a celestial being (Dan. 10:13, 21; 12:1; Jude 9; Rev. 12:7). He is nowhere explicitly identified with Jesus, but some Christian writers have equated the two by carefully comparing the role played by Michael with that of Jesus. Any comparisons yield not only similarities but also dissimilarities, and both should be taken into account. We'll start with the passages in which Michael is mentioned and then broaden the horizon to include several passages that are conceptually related to His person and experience.

1. He seems to be an angel: Michael is identified as "one of the chief princes" (Dan. 10:13), "your prince" (verse 21), "the great prince" (Dan. 12:1), and "the archangel" (Jude 9). "Archangel" implies that He is the prince of the angels, suggesting that Michael cannot be another name for Jesus, because He is divine and angels are created beings.

Part of the problem is that the noun *angel* is taken to designate a creature, while in the Bible it designates a function. In other words, an "angel" is a being who functions as a "messenger" of God. In most cases they are created beings, but there is an exception.

In the Old Testament there are several references to the "angel [messenger] of the Lord" in which He is equated with God (e.g., Ex. 3:2, 4;

Judges 6:12, 14). It is not that the Messenger is identified with the One who sent Him as His representative, but rather that the Sender functions at the same time as the Messenger. Many Christians have identified the Angel of the Lord as the preincarnate Christ. This Christological interpretation seems to be biblically valid.

2. He is leader of the angels: The phrase *one of the chief princes* (Dan. 10:13) could give the impression that He is one among many princes. But according to Revelation 12:7, Michael is the supreme leader of the heavenly angels, or "the great prince." When necessary, He personally assists angels in their assigned tasks (Dan. 10:13), yet the angelic hosts are under His command (Rev. 12:7). He is indeed the "archangel" (Jude 9). This title is mentioned in one other place in the Bible: 1 Thessalonians 4:16, in the context of the Second Coming of Christ. He returns "with the voice of the archangel," suggesting that Michael is most probably another name for Jesus.

3. He protects God's people: Michael is described as the Prince of Israel (Dan. 10:21), the One who protects Israel (Dan. 12:1). This protection is described in military terms and portrays the Prince as a warrior. In practically all the passages in which He is mentioned there is a conflict between God's people and their enemies, and Michael is present to defend them or fight for them. The protection can also take the form of judgment, in which Michael stands up and defends and delivers God's people *(Ibid.).* Those are functions of Christ in the New Testament and confirm the suggestion that Michael and Christ are the same person, involved in leadership in the heavenly and earthly realms.

4. He is Prince of the heavenly hosts: In Daniel 8:10 there is a reference to a celestial being who performs the daily services in the heavenly sanctuary. There is only one other passage in the Old Testament in which this being is mentioned. Joshua had an encounter with a being who identified himself as the "captain [commander] of the host [army] of the Lord" (Joshua 5:14). He ordered Joshua to remove his shoes because the ground he was standing on was holy, similar to God's apparition to Moses. The context makes clear that this being was the Lord Himself (Joshua 6:2). This Prince is the same person called in other passages Prince Michael, and therefore we can identify Him with the preincarnate Christ.

So even though the Bible does not clearly identify Michael with Christ, there is enough biblical information to warrant the view that They are the same person. The name *Michael* stresses the fact that Christ is the supreme leader of the heavenly angels and the defender of His people as warrior, judge, and priest.

CHEIROGRAPHON TOIS DOGMASIN

Correspondence on the Sabbath Question

Alan, I looked over your website and liked what I saw. I noticed on your Ministry Profile page what you said about your commitment to God's Word. I like the fact that you base your ministry on the conviction that the Bible is the very Word of God—the final authority for all that Christians believe and do. So I have a question for you. I am assuming that you believe in the creation account found in Genesis. In Genesis 2:3 it says: "And God blessed the seventh day, and made it holy because on it He ceased from all the work that He had been doing in creation." My question is this: on what date did God rescind that blessing and remove holiness from Saturday?

John Witcombe

Dear John, It has been a long time since I have had opportunity to review Scriptures regarding the Sabbath and related issues. We both know there has been much debate on this subject since the earliest days of the church. The simple answer to your question is God did not rescind that blessing. **The question which remains is how does that blessing apply to Saturday, in light of additional biblical passages and statements?**

Dear Alan, thank you for your response. I would like to respond to "the question which remains," which was: "How does that blessing apply to Saturday, in light of additional biblical passages and statements?" First of all, any interpretation of the additional Bible passages must pass the litmus test that is to be used to test all truth: "To the law and to the testimony: if they speak not according to this word, it is because there is no light in them." Isaiah 8:20.

For instance, if I thought that Paul was approving murder because of the way I interpreted Galatians 5:12—"I would they were even cut off which trouble you"—then either my interpretation of that text is wrong or else Paul was a false prophet, because approving murder violates commandment six, which says, "Thou shalt not kill." If Paul ever wrote anything that would change one jot or one tittle of the moral law that God wrote with His own finger—if he wrote anything that would suggest that Christians no longer need to literally obey the particulars of any one of the Ten Commandments—there would be no light in him.

However, I know there is light in the writings of Paul, because he upholds the Law of God. "Wherefore the law is holy, and the commandment holy, and just, and good." Romans 7:12. "For not the hearers of the law are just before God, but the doers of the law shall be justified." Romans 2:13. "Circumcision is nothing, and uncircumcision is nothing. Instead, keeping God's commandments is what counts." 1 Corinthians 7:19.

Now there are some writings of Paul that, on the surface, appear to downplay the importance of the law of God and keeping holy the seventh-day Sabbath of the fourth commandment. Peter may have had these passages in mind when he wrote: "As also in all his epistles, speaking in them of these things; in which are some things hard to be understood, which they that are unlearned and unstable wrest, as they do also the other scriptures, unto their own destruction." 2 Peter 3:16.

Each Pauline passage that is used to show that Christians no longer need to keep the seventh-day Sabbath holy according to the directives of the fourth commandment has a very sensible and biblical interpretation that allows that passage to fall within God's litmus test of truth—"To the law and to the testimony."

For instance, Colossians 2:14-17 is a passage that is often used to show that the moral law together with the Sabbath was nailed to the Cross. But is that what Paul was actually saying? If he was, then he fails the biblical test.

Colossians 2:14-17: "Blotting out the **handwriting of ordinances** that was **against us, which was contrary to us**, and took it out of the way, nailing it to his cross; [And] having spoiled principalities and powers, he made a show of them openly, triumphing over them in it. Let no man therefore judge you in meat, or in drink, or in respect of an holyday, or of the new moon, or of the sabbath [days]: Which are a shadow of things to come; but the body [is] of Christ."

The question to be answered is what is "handwriting of ordinances"? Since the word *handwriting* or *cheirographon* occurs only this once in Scripture, we must first ask of the text, "*cheirographon*, or handwriting—of what"? After all, handwriting can be a handwriting about anything. Handwriting? What other kind of writing was there back then? Today when we talk about a handwritten note, it is to contrast it with a type-written one. Back then, when it came to the law, there was one that was handwritten—the ceremonial law—and one that was "finger-written"—the Moral Law. "And the LORD delivered unto me two tables of stone written with the finger of God" Deuteronomy 9:10.

So we should ask, handwriting, of what? The answer from the text is *cheirographon tois dogmasin*—"handwriting of ordinances." What is *dogma*, or *dogmasin*? We are familiar with "dogma" in our language—church dogmatics, for example, means dogmatic, or strong, authoritative, teaching or doctrines about the church, or having to do with the church.

Paul was acquainted with the terminology used in the Old Testament. He no doubt knew the book of Deuteronomy very well. He was aware that there were two laws given to Israel. First, there was the Ten Commandment law of God, written by the finger of God. Second, there was the body of law and instruction which God communicated to Moses, including the ceremonial law, which Moses wrote with his own hand.

Of this body of law, we read: "And Moses wrote this law, and delivered it unto the priests the sons of Levi, which bare the ark of the covenant of the Lord and unto all the elders of Israel. And Moses commanded them, saying, At the end of every seven years, in the solemnity of the year of release, in the feast of tabernacles, When all Israel is come to appear before the Lord thy God in the place which he shall choose, thou shall read this law before all Israel in their hearing. . . . And it came to pass, when Moses had made an end of writing the words of this law in a book, until they were finished, That Moses commanded the Levites, which bare the ark of the covenant of the Lord, saying, Take this book of the law, and put it in the side of the ark of the covenant of the Lord your God, that it may be there for a **witness against thee**. For I know thy rebellion, and thy stiff neck: behold, while I am yet alive with you this day, ye have been rebellious against the Lord; and how much more after my death?" Deut. 31:9-11; 24-27.

Notice, the very expression *against* used by Paul in Colossians 2:14 was used by Moses in Deuteronomy 31. Moses wrote, with his own hand, ordinances which were to be read every seven years in the year of release to all Israel. Moses told them to put this handwritten law in the side of the ark that it "may be there for a witness against thee."

Clearly, in the mind of Paul, steeped in the Old Testament, the handwriting of ordinances is this very handwriting of Moses spoken of in Deuteronomy 31, called the book of the law, placed in the side of the Ark that it might be there for a witness against Israel.

Look at the word *ordinances*. That word occurs over in Ephesians 2:15: "Having abolished in his flesh the enmity, the law of commandments in ordinances [dogmasin]; for to make in himself of twain one new man, so making peace."

The word sequence in Greek is interesting: "The law of commandments in dogmasin He invalidated, nullified, annulled, made of no effect, in order that of the two He might create in Him one, one new man, making peace." Eph. 2:15 (Gr. Trans.). Here in this passage, parallel with Col. 2:14, we find what happened to the ordinances: Christ nullified, annulled, the law of commandments in ordinances, the ceremonial law, in order that of the two, Gentile and Hebrew—one outside the law; the other with the law—He might make one of the two.

The ceremonial law had been used by the Jews to build up a barrier between Jew and Greek. This, Christ took out of the way, nullifying it, so that He could create the Church, made up of both Jew and Greek. The context of Ephesians 2:15 shows the whole picture.

1. Eph. 2:11: "You being in time past Gentiles in the flesh, who are called Uncircumcision by that which is called the Circumcision in the flesh made by hands." Here is the division: Uncircumcision vs. Circumcision.

2. Eph. 2:12: "Without Christ, being aliens from the commonwealth of Israel, and strangers from the covenants of promise, having no hope, and without God in the world." The Uncircumcised were aliens from the commonwealth of Israel, strangers from the covenants of promise. They were outsiders. There was a barrier: *Circumcision,* a term which stands for the whole ceremonial law, vs. *Uncircumcision,* standing for those outside the commonwealth of Israel, beyond the pale of hope.

3. Eph. 2:13: "But now, through the blood of Christ, in Christ those who were sometimes far off are made nigh by the blood of Christ." The blood of Christ takes away the barrier. No longer is the path to God through the ceremonial law which marked the Jews as the

commonwealth of Israel. Now the issue is the blood of Christ, which alone brings the believer near.

4. Eph. 2:14: "He [Christ] is our peace, who hath made both one, and hath broken down the middle wall of partition."

5. Eph. 2:15: "Having abolished in His flesh the enmity, the law of commandments in ordinances; for to make in Himself of twain one new man, so making peace."

In Colossians 2:14, Paul further explains what He was talking about when he says "handwriting of ordinances" by mentioning a series of things in the verses that follow: Meat (offerings), drink (offerings) holydays (days of holy convocations), new moons, or sabbaths (the Levitical, shadowy sabbaths of Lev. 23) "which are a shadow of things to come, but the body is of Christ." All of this series is mentioned in Leviticus 23.

The Passover/Unleavened Bread feast, for example, involved holydays (v. 8), sacrifice of the Paschal lamb (v. 12), meat offering (v. 13), drink offering (v. 13); the Day of Atonement involved a Levitical sabbath (v. 32); the Feast of Tabernacles, or Booths, involved Levitical sabbaths (v. 39). The new moons are mentioned throughout Chronicles, Ezra, Nehemiah, Isaiah, Ezekiel, Hosea, and Amos.

Paul's list in Colossians 2:16 involved the ceremonial observances which Daniel's prophecy (Dan. 9:27) declared Christ would cause to cease in the midst of the week, A.D. 31, at His crucifixion. "In the midst of the week He shall cause the sacrifice (slaughtering, victim, meal, repast) and the oblation (present, gift; tribute; sacrifice [mostly an unbloody one], offering) to cease." Daniel 9:27 (Heb. Amp. Tr.). To show that the ceremonial law with its temple services had come to an end, the veil of the temple was rent when Christ died. "And behold, the veil of the temple was rent in twain from the top to the bottom." Matt.27:51.

Not only does Paul list the sabbaths in a series of ceremonial elements—meat (offerings), or in drink (offerings), or in respect of an holyday, or of the new moon, or of the sabbaths, but in the very next clause of the next verse Paul tells even more clearly just what sabbaths he was speaking of—the Levitical, ceremonial sabbaths of the ceremonial law. Paul says: "which are a **shadow** of things to come."

The Levitical sabbaths of Leviticus 23 which were a part of the Feast of Trumpets, of the Day of Atonement service, the Feast of Tabernacles, etc., fell on any day of the week and specifically pointed forward to the reality in Christ, as did the rest of the ceremonial law. But the seventh-day Sabbath of the Ten Commandments is part of the moral law. It was established in Eden before man sinned as a commemoration of the creation of this world—not as a shadow of things to come. Several Bible commentaries support this interpretation:

Adam Clarke's Commentary: Verse 16. Let no man judge you in meat, or in drink . . . and the necessity of observing certain holydays or festivals, such as the new moons and particular sabbaths, or those which should be observed with more than ordinary solemnity; all these had been taken out of the way and nailed to the cross, and were no longer of moral obligation. There is no intimation here that the Sabbath was done away, or that its moral use was superseded, by the introduction of Christianity. I have shown elsewhere that, Remember the Sabbath day, to keep it holy, is a command of perpetual obligation, and can never be superseded but by the final termination of time. (**Albert Barnes' New Testament Commentary, Family Bible Notes, and Jamieson, Fausset & Brown's Commentary** all agree.)

Alan, in your comments, you said, "New Testament teaching allows for a good deal of latitude when it comes to the individual's appreciation of this matter of the Sabbath (taking a day off to rest from all labor; resting in the finished work of Christ), as one man may honor one day above another, and the next man may honor all days alike before the Lord. No believer is to act as another man's judge, when it comes to the specific day, or days that an individual chooses to honor the Lord. It is essential that each person be fully convinced in his own mind."

If we believe that Paul is allowing a good deal of latitude when it comes to whether or not one keeps the seventh-day Sabbath as specified in the fourth commandment, then we put Paul at odds with the law of God. Paul is not referencing the Sabbath of the fourth commandment when he is speaking of honoring one day above another in Romans 14:5. From the context it appears that Paul is most likely referring to practices of abstinence and fasting on regular fixed dates. A couple of Bible commentaries that I have on my Power Bible CD software interpret this text in a way that keeps the writings of Paul in line with the litmus test of Isaiah 8:20:

Family Bible Notes on Romans 14:5: "The apostle here has no reference to the difference of days spoken of in the moral law."

Adam Clarke's Commentary on Romans 14:5: "One man esteemeth one day above another." We add here alike, and make the text say what I am sure was never intended, viz. that there is no distinction of days, not even of the Sabbath: and that every Christian is at liberty to consider even this day to be holy or not holy, as he happens to be persuaded in his own mind."

Alan, you are the second Bible scholar that I have posed my question to. Here is the correspondence I had with the first Bible scholar:

Ralph, here's a question for you to give thoughtful consideration to. "And God blessed the seventh day, and made it holy because on it He ceased from all the work that He had been doing in creation." Genesis 2:3. **On what date did God rescind that blessing and remove holiness from Saturday?**

Ralph responds: "True Bible students understand that the Sabbath rest signifies spiritually much more than simply resting from work on Saturday. In the New Testament the Sabbath changed in significance and changed in how we keep it. There is your answer."

Ralph, you said: "True Bible students understand that the Sabbath rest signifies spiritually much more than simply resting from work on Saturday." This is true Ralph, but wouldn't it at least include resting as it says God did in Exodus 20:11? "For in six days the LORD made heaven and earth, the sea, and all that in them is, and rested the seventh day: wherefore the LORD blessed the Sabbath day, and hallowed it." Resting did not diminish the spiritual lessons Adam, Moses, or Paul received from the Sabbath. Resting as commanded in the Law of God would only enhance the spiritual significance for the true Bible student.

Consider this: God established the holy Sabbath day before sin entered this world just as He established the institution of marriage before the fall of man. After sin God uses the Sabbath day rest to symbolize the rest we receive when we accept Jesus as our Saviour (Heb. 4:10). He also uses marriage to represent the relationship of His church to himself (Eph. 5:32). The fact that marriage is used to illustrate spiritual truth does not mean we abandon the institution and cohabit with multiple individuals. Now that marriage is used to illustrate spiritual reality it is even more important to follow the exact guidelines God has laid down for marriage. So it is with the Sabbath.

The Sabbath was given to man to be a weekly reminder that it was God that made us, not we ourselves. When God made the Sabbath there was no old covenant, there was no new covenant, there were no Jews; the Sabbath predates the giving of the law at Mount Sinai. The Sabbath was not a temporary institution to be kept until Christ should be crucified. If the Sabbath had been made after man sinned then it could be argued that it was perhaps a shadow of something to come and therefore only temporary as was the sacrificial service. However, the Sabbath is foremost a memorial to the fact that God is Creator. Just because Jesus was resurrected on Sunday does not diminish the fact that He is our Creator and that He established the Holy Sabbath day as a memorial to that fact.

You can assemble to worship God on Sunday to honor His resurrection or on Friday to commemorate His crucifixion, or on Thursday to remember His last supper with His disciples. We do not make these days holy by our assembling together. Only a holy God can make something holy. And only He can remove holiness from something He has made holy. The Bible clearly tells us when He made the Sabbath holy and it would just as clearly have to tell us that there was no longer a need to have a memorial to creation. With the teaching of evolution so widespread, the Sabbath becomes even more important as a weekly reminder that we did not evolve but were created by a loving Creator. Jesus did in fact institute a memorial to His resurrection. It was not an additional holy day but rather He gave us baptism and the Lord's Supper to commemorate His death, burial and resurrection.

Ralph responds: "By faith the Biblical Old Testament believers accepted and carried out God's law. Likewise, we New Testament believers by faith accept the Lamb of God and in Him all the Law and the prophecies were fulfilled. Obeying the law is not what makes us righteous. I believe that Jesus fulfilled the law and so its power over us passed away."

Ralph, I agree that the law cannot make us righteous. The law only informs us whether or not we are acting in a righteous way. The power to act in a righteous way can only come from God, not the law. Apart from Christ, we cannot obey the law because it is "holy, just and good" (Rom. 7:12). Only those whom God makes holy can keep holy that which is holy. "Because it is written, Be ye holy; for I am holy." 1 Peter 1:16. Man by himself is not capable of holiness. But "I can do all things through Christ who strengthens me." Phil. 4:13. The solution to sin is not to destroy the law. The solution is an indwelling Christ who empowers us to obey His commandments. Jesus said: "Think not that I am come to destroy the law, or the prophets: I am not come to destroy, but to fulfill. Matt. 5:17. Jesus fulfilled the law in the same manner as He fulfilled all righteousness. "And Jesus answering said unto him, Suffer it to be so now: for thus it becometh us to fulfill all righteousness." Matt. 3:15. To fulfill all righteousness does not mean to alter or do away with righteousness. It means to carry out, perform, or discharge. That is how Christ fulfilled the law.

Now He wants to fulfill that law in us. "That the righteousness of the law might be fulfilled in us." Romans 8:4.

God promises to write His law in our hearts and cause us to walk in them (Eze. 36:26, 27). Obedience to the law of God is not our love gift to God but rather it is God's love gift to us. "For this is the love of God, that we keep his commandments: and his commandments are not grievous" 1 John 5:3. The commands of the law are not terrible; rather they are promises of the kind of behavior we can expect when Christ lives in us. Remember, He is doing the work in us; therefore, we cannot boast. God promises: we shall not curse, lie, steal, kill, covet, commit adultery, profane His Sabbath, etc. Thus we are no longer under the law, that is, under the condemnation of law, but under grace for it is the powerful indwelling grace of God that frees us from the condemnation disobedience to God's law brings. The Apostle James calls the Ten Commandments the law of liberty: "For whosoever shall keep the whole law, and yet offend in one point, he is guilty of all. For he that said, Do not commit adultery, said also, Do not kill. Now if thou commit no adultery, yet if thou kill, thou art become a transgressor of the law. So speak ye, and so do, as they that shall be judged by the law of liberty." James 2:10-12.

The law of God is eternal (Ps. 111:7, 8). It was written in the hearts of God's children before it was codified at Mount Sinai. Scripture says that Abraham kept the Law of God. "Abraham obeyed my voice, kept my charge, my commandments, my statutes, and my laws." Gen. 26:5. Joseph knew not to fornicate. These and more show us the existence of a moral law. In contrast to the Mosaic laws which were to pass away someday, the law of God was eternal and would never pass away.

God required Israel to keep His laws before Sinai. "And the Lord said unto to Moses, How long refuse ye to keep my commandments and my laws. So the people rested on the Seventh day." Ex.16:28. God expected His people to keep the Sabbath before Sinai at which point the law was written in stone. Before Sinai, God gave them a double portion of manna on Friday. Why? So they could keep the Sabbath holy with Him, according to the commandment. (Ex.16: 25-30).

Satan hates God's law and has convinced men that God is not particular anymore in regards to it. Especially has he attacked the Sabbath which is a weekly reminder that God is our mighty Creator. But the Sabbath remains blessed and holy in spite of what man thinks. Even in the earth made new the redeemed will remember to keep the Sabbath day holy: "For as the new heavens and the new earth, which I will make, shall remain before me, saith the LORD, so shall your seed and your name remain. And it shall come to pass, that from one new moon to another, and from one Sabbath to another, shall all flesh come to worship before me, saith the LORD." Isa. 66:22, 23.

John Witcombe

THE BEAST AND HIS MARK

This subject is one of the most important in the Bible. Who is the antichrist beast? And what is his mark?

The most serious warning God sends to the world in the last days is found in Revelation 14:9, 10:

"And the third angel followed them, saying with a loud voice, 'If any man worship the beast and his image, and receive his mark in his forehead, or in his hand, The same shall drink of the wine of the wrath of God, which is poured out without mixture into the cup of his indignation; and he shall be tormented with fire and brimstone in the presence of the holy angels, and in the presence of the Lamb.'"

All who worship the beast, or worship its image, or receive the mark of the beast will be toast. We know that God loves us, and if He has sent such a serious message, we can be certain that He has also made it abundantly clear who and what this beast represents.

Let's go to Revelation 13 and read about this beast power that God has warned us about:

"And I stood upon the sand of the sea, and saw a beast rise up out of the sea, having seven heads and ten horns, and upon his horns ten crowns, and upon his heads the name of blasphemy. And the beast which I saw was like unto a leopard, and his feet were as the feet of a bear, and his mouth as the mouth of a lion: and the dragon gave him his power, and his seat, and great authority. And I saw one of his heads as it were wounded to death; and his deadly wound was healed: and all the world wondered after the beast."—Revelation 13:1-3.

Now, this is a strange beast! Is this a literal animal? No, it is obviously symbolic—it represents something. The Bible tells us what it is. Let's get the Bible interpretation of each part.

First, it comes from the water or sea. What does *water* symbolize? In Revelation 17:15, we find the answer: "And he saith unto me, 'The waters which thou sawest, where the whore sitteth, are peoples, and multitudes, and nations, and tongues.'" The *waters* or *sea* always symbolizes many nations of people that speak different languages.

Now what about those other strange parts—body of a leopard, feet of a bear, head of a lion, and ten horns? We must go to the book of Daniel in the Old Testament to understand. Daniel and Revelation explain each other. You cannot understand one book without the other—keys are in each. So we will spend a little time in Daniel, and you will see something amazing when we go back to Revelation 13.

Let's look at Daniel 7. Here we have another prophetic vision: "Daniel spake and said, 'I saw in my vision by night, and, behold the four winds of the heaven strove upon the great sea. And four great beasts came up from the *sea*, diverse one from another.'"—Daniel 7:2, 3, emphasis supplied. Remember, *water* or *seas* represents multitudes of people.

Then verse 3 says that "four great beasts came up." What do beasts represent in prophecy? The answer is in verse 17: "These great beasts, which are four, are four kings, which shall arise out of the earth." Then verse 23 says: "Thus he said, 'The fourth beast shall be the *fourth kingdom* upon the earth, which shall be diverse from all kingdoms, and shall devour the whole earth, and shall tread it down, and break it in pieces.'"—emphasis supplied. That means the first four beasts represent the first four kings and their kingdoms.

We still follow this practice today—animals representing kingdoms. There is the American eagle, the Russian bear, the Chinese dragon, etc. Let's look closer at these kingdoms.

First Kingdom

"The first was like a lion, and had eagle's wings: I beheld till the wings thereof were plucked, and it was lifted up from the earth, and made stand upon the feet as a man, and a man's heart was given to it."—Daniel 7:4.

Who was this first world empire? Babylon—represented by the king of beasts. Wings, in prophecy, represent speed (Habakkuk 1:8). The prophecy begins with Babylon—the kingdom Daniel is living in. In the Bible,

Babylon is referred to as a lion (compare 2 Kings 24:1; Jeremiah 51:37, 38). As the ruins of Babylon have been excavated, we see still today many winged lions carved on the walls of that ancient city. Babylon ruled from 606 B.C. to 538 B.C.

Second Kingdom

"And behold another beast, a second, like to a bear, and it raised up itself on one side, and it had three ribs in the mouth of it between the teeth of it: and they said thus unto it, 'Arise, devour much flesh.'"—Daniel 7:5.

Here is the second world empire—Medo-Persia, raised up on one side. It came up as a joint empire; however, the Persians were stronger than the Medes. The three ribs symbolize the three Babylonian provinces it conquered of the then-known world—Babylonia, Egypt, and Lydia. Medo-Persia ruled from 538 B.C. to 331 B.C.

Third Kingdom

"After this I beheld, and lo another, like a leopard, which had upon the back of it four wings of a fowl; the beast had also four heads; and dominion was given to it."—Daniel 7:6.

In 331 B.C. the third beast arose. It had four wings representing double speed, a fitting expression of the swiftness of Alexander the Great, who quickly conquered the world and established the empire of Greece. The four heads represent the four temporary kingdoms that were formed after Alexander's death, divided by his four top generals. The Northern territory went to Lysimachus; the South to Ptolemy; the East to Seleucus; and the West to Cassander. Greece ruled from 331 B.C. to 168 B.C.

Fourth Kingdom

"After this I saw in the night visions, and behold a fourth beast, dreadful and terrible, and strong exceedingly; and it had great iron teeth: it devoured and brake in pieces, and stamped the residue with the feet of it: and it was diverse from all the beasts that were before it; and it had ten horns."—Daniel 7:7.

The fourth beast was strange. Daniel had never seen anything like this! He knew a lion, a leopard, and a bear, but this was unique! The dreadful fourth beast was the fourth kingdom:

"Thus he said, 'The fourth beast shall be the fourth kingdom upon the earth, which shall be diverse from all the kingdoms, and shall devour the whole earth, and shall tread it down, and break it in pieces.'"—Daniel 7:23.

All four kingdoms occupied the same territory. What kingdom conquered Greece and took over its territory? The fourth kingdom unquestionably represents Rome, which ruled from 168 B.C. to A.D. 476.

What about the ten horns on this fourth beast? Let's see what they represent:

"And the ten horns out of this kingdom are ten kings that shall arise: and another shall rise after them; and he shall be diverse from the first, and he shall subdue three kings."—Daniel 7:24.

The ten horns are ten kings or kingdoms. When Rome fell, it was divided into ten parts as the barbarian tribes swept in. Those ten tribes were the Alamanni (Germany), the Visigoths (Spain), the Franks (France), the Suevi (Portugal), the Burgundians (Switzerland), the Anglo Saxons (England), and the Lombards (Italy). Three of the tribes no longer exist: the Ostrogoths, the Vandals, and the Heruli. To find out why they do not exist, let's read Daniel 7:8:

"I considered the horns, and, behold, there came up among them another *little horn*, before whom there were *three* of the first horns plucked up by the roots: and, behold, in this horn [little horn] were eyes like the eyes of man, and a mouth speaking great things."—emphasis supplied.

Suddenly, there comes up another *little horn* or little kingdom.

These three kingdoms were destroyed by another little kingdom arising. Now, who is the little horn? If you really wanted to know, you could ask your history teacher, and he could probably tell you what kingdom destroyed the Ostrogoths, Vandals, and Heruli. We're going to discover a lot about the little horn as we go on. You will see that this little horn kingdom is the antichrist power—the same as the beast power God warns us about in Revelation 13.

Now, we must be very careful and clear in identifying this kingdom and power. And God has done just that. In the next few verses God will give us nine marks of identification as to who this power is so that we don't need to guess at this. He makes it so clear that there is no room for speculation. God gives nine marks and these nine apply to no power in history but one.

Nine Identifying Points

1. This power comes up *among them* (Daniel 7:8). So now we have it located geographically. The other ten horns, or kingdoms, were in Western Europe. So if it comes up *among them,* it would have to be a little kingdom that comes up somewhere in Western Europe.

2. If it came up *among them,* it had to come up after the year A.D. 476, because the ten kingdoms were not there until A.D. 476 after Rome, the fourth beast, fell.

3. It would be a *little horn* (Daniel 7:8) or a little kingdom. Not a big empire like the others, but it begins as a little one.

4. It *uproots three kingdoms* (Daniel 7:8). We have already established that the Ostrogoths, Vandals, and Heruli were these three kingdoms.

5. It was *diverse* or different (Daniel 7:24). How? It would not be a government like the others but different from any system ever before.

6. It would *speak great words* (Daniel 7:25). Revelation 13:5 says *great words and blasphemy.* Let's get two Bible definitions of blasphemy. John 10:31-33 says blasphemy is when a man claims to be God. Mark 2:5-7 says blasphemy is when a man claims to have the power to forgive sins. So this *man* at the head of this kingdom would do this.

7. It would *wear out the saints* (Daniel 7:25). This power would fight against God, against God's people, and be a persecuting power. God's people would be martyred and slain by it.

8. He would *think to change times and laws* (Daniel 7:25). This power would *think* and try to do away with God's holy times and laws. That can't be done, but this power would *think to* and try to change them.

9. Daniel 7:25 tells us how long it would rule. It would rule for a "time, times, and dividing of time." Now, this is a prophetic term. The Bible tells us how long it is, though. If we compare Revelation 12:14 and 12:6, we find that it equals 1260 days. That means: *time* is one year, *times* is two years and the *dividing of time* is a half a year—the total is three and a half years. How many days are in

three and a half years using the Bible calendar of thirty days to a month? Twelve hundred and sixty days.

Now, here's another key of prophecy. Remember that in prophecy we are dealing with symbols. A *day* is also symbolic. It is symbolic of a year (Ezekiel 4:6; Numbers 14:34). Whenever God spoke prophetically as in these texts, the day-for-a-year principle was followed. (Note that this applies only in prophetic Scripture.) So this power will rule for 1260 days, or years. We have nine points. All these came from the Bible alone!

You can probably guess what power the little horn or antichrist beast is already. The fact is that there is one and only one power that meets these nine requirements. God is precise. However, God also wants us to realize that He is talking about a system, a kingdom, *not sincere people who may be a part of the system*. Truth is not against sincere people. Truth is against error. God loves us and gives these nine points so we will not be deceived. It is indisputably clear that these points apply to one power only in the history of the world, and that is the papacy. Now, notice that God is not speaking of Catholic Church members in a derogatory way. There are many priests, nuns, and Catholic people who love the Lord with all their hearts and have dedicated their lives in service to humanity. There are good, sincere people in all churches. God simply identifies the political kingdom of the papacy because like all nations it had a very significant history with the Christian church. Before we go into that, though, let's take a closer look at the nine points to see how they apply.

Application of Identifying Points

1. and 2. Daniel 7:8: It "came up among" the other ten horns or kingdoms, after A.D. 476. There is only one "little" kingdom that fits this description and that's the Vatican City and the Holy Roman Empire.

3. Daniel 7:8: It is still to this day in some ways a "little" kingdom. The Vatican is only 109 acres in size. But it is now a powerful kingdom and the wealthiest kingdom in the world. No other power fits this description.

4. Daniel 7:8: It "uproots three kingdoms." Clearly documented in history is the eradication of the Heruli, Vandals, and Ostrogoths by the armies of papal Rome. The last to go were the Ostrogoths in A.D. 538. The same year, the Roman Emperor Justinian gave the Bishop of Rome authority over the kingdom.

5. Daniel 7:24: It would be "diverse," or different. All the preceding

kingdoms had been simple governments set up in a normal political manner. Papal Rome, however, was and still is unique and different because it is a *church* that rules. Policies are dictated by the bishops and popes.

6. Daniel 7:25: It speaks "great words," or blasphemy. The Bible definition of blasphemy is composed of two things: (1) A man claiming to be God. (2) A man claiming to have power to forgive sins. There is only one power today that fits that description—the papal power. Let's get documented proof of this from the pages of Catholic sources. We'll look at some older ones as well as sources from our day. Please note that we'll look at multiple sources, as it is important to see clearly and fairly that the Roman Church fits this sixth identifying characteristic.

In *Ferraris' Ecclesiastical Dictionary*, Prompta Bibliothica (Handy Library), vol. 6, 1858, under an article entitled *Pope*, we read the following:

> "The Pope is of so great dignity and so exalted that he is not a man, but as it were, God, and the Vicar of God. The Pope is called 'Most Holy' because he is rightfully presumed to be such.... He is likewise the divine Monarch and supreme Emperor, and King of Kings.... The Pope is as it were God on earth, sole sovereign of the faithful of Christ, chief king of kings, having plenitude of power."

Much of official Catholic doctrine is taken from the numerous ecumenical councils that have taken place over the centuries. "Ecumenical" means that Catholic leaders from around the world gathered to determine what the church would do and teach. The First Vatican Council took place in 1869 and 1870. In the fourth session of that council on July 18, 1870, in the section entitled "First Dogmatic Constitution on the Church of Christ," chapter 3, we find the following words: [Note: This quotation and others to follow have been shortened for the sake of space only. For the full text, see the two-volume *Decrees of the Ecumenical Councils*, edited by Norman P. Tanner, S.J., and published through Sheed & Ward and the Georgetown University Press in 1990.]

> "...the Roman pontiff is the...head of the whole church and father and teacher of all Christian people.... The Roman church possesses a pre-eminence of ordinary power over every other church.... Both clergy and faithful are bound to submit to this power.... In this way, by unity with the Roman pontiff in communion and in profession of the same faith, the church of Christ becomes one flock under one supreme shepherd. (Tanner, pages 813 and 814)."

These words are in direct conflict with Scripture. The Bible clearly states that *Christ* is the head of the church (Ephesians 4:15), not the pope;

that *Christ* is the supreme shepherd (1 Peter 5:4), not the pope. Thus, the pope in essence claims to be God, for he takes on himself characteristics that only belong to God.

Moreover, the papacy also claims that the pope is infallible—that is—that he cannot make a mistake in decisions regarding church-wide doctrine and therefore is to be obeyed implicitly. Again, witness the words of the fourth chapter of "First Dogmatic Constitution on the Church of Christ," given at the First Vatican Council:

> "...when the Roman pontiff speaks *ex cathedra*, that is...when he defines a doctrine concerning faith or morals to be held by the whole church, he possesses...infallibility...(Tanner, page 816)."

This doctrine of papal infallibility is blasphemy, for God alone is infallible. To say that the pope, a mere man, can be absolutely correct and must therefore be obeyed when he makes decrees on how the entire Christian church should believe and act is against clear biblical teaching to the contrary. The Roman church "anathematizes" (that is, condemns to hell) anyone who refuses to accept the pope's infallibility (see First Vatican Council, fourth session, July 18, 1870, in the section entitled "First Dogmatic Constitution on the Church of Christ," end of chapter 3/Tanner, pages 814, 815).

The Roman Church reaffirmed papal infallibility and all Christians' duty to obey the pope at the Second Vatican Council in the 1960s (see the section entitled *Lumen Gentum*, 25/Tanner page 869), and it remains official Catholic doctrine today. Witness the following quotation from the current *Catechism of the Catholic Church*, sections 937 and 891:

> "The Pope enjoys, by divine institution, 'supreme, full, immediate, and universal power in the care of souls.'" (937)

> "The Roman Pontiff, head of the college of bishops, enjoys this infallibility, when...he proclaims by a definitive act a doctrine pertaining to faith or morals.... [These] definitions must be adhered to...." (891)

With these current statements in mind, older statements such as the following from *La Civila Cattolica* (The Catholic Civilization), a periodical founded by the Jesuits in 1850 in Naples, Italy, that is still being published today, are seen to reflect current Catholic teaching in spite of their age:

> "The Pope is the supreme judge of the law of the land.... He is the vicegerent of Christ, and is not only a priest forever, but also king of kings and Lord of lords." (March 18, 1871).

"The Pope is not only the representative of Jesus Christ, but he is Jesus Christ, Himself, hidden under the veil of flesh."—*Catholic National*, July, 1895.

Does the pope claim to be God? Yes, both directly and through his taking on himself attributes that can only belong to God.

What about the claim to be able to forgive sins?

"The priest does really and truly forgive sins in virtue of the power given to him by Christ."—*Joseph Deharbe's Catechism*, page 279.

"Seek where you will, through heaven and earth, and you will find but one created being who can forgive the sinner, who can free him from the chains of hell; that extraordinary being is the priest, the [Roman] Catholic priest. Yes, beloved brethren, the priest not only declares that the sinner is forgiven, but he really forgives him. The priest raises his hand, he pronounces the word of absolution, and in an instant, quick as a flash of light the chains of hell are burst asunder, and the sinner becomes a child of God. So great is the power of the priest that the judgments of heaven itself are subject to his decision."—Michael Muller, *The Catholic Priest*, pages 78, 79.

And from the current *Catechism of the Catholic Church*, sections 1461 and 1484, we find the following:

"Indeed bishops and priests, by virtue of the sacrament of Holy Orders, have the power to forgive all sins..." (1461)

"Individual, integral confession [to a priest] and absolution [from a priest] remain the only ordinary way for the faithful to reconcile themselves with God..." (1484)

Truly, no other power on earth can fulfill this identifying point.

7. Daniel 7:25: He would war against God's people and persecute them. Although this is now past, all people of the earth are aware of the millions of martyrs put to death during the Dark Ages by the Papal armies. The most conservative estimates are that 50 million men and women were put to death. One needs only to read the pages of hundreds of history books available to document this. Pope Innocent III, 1198-1216, was responsible for thousands of martyrs. The Spanish Inquisition, the Massacre of St. Bartholomew, and the history of the Waldenses are a few examples. We do not cite this for the purpose of casting aspersions. These things are past; however, we must discuss them to see the fulfillment of prophecy.

8. Daniel 7:25: He would "think to change times and laws." In the *Convert's Catechism of Catholic Doctrine*, page 49, we find that God's law has been changed. Exodus 20 contains God's law as He wrote it with His own finger in stone. However, the law as printed in the *Convert's Catechism* has omitted the second commandment and split the tenth in two. (The current *Catechism of the Catholic Church* does nearly the same: Compare section 2084 with 2142, and section 2514 with 2534.) Ferraris' *Catholic Ecclesiastical Dictionary* goes so far as to say that:

> "The pope is of so great authority and power that he can modify, change, or interpret even divine laws. The pope can modify divine law, since his power is not of man but of God, and he acts as vicegerent of God upon the earth with most ample power of binding and loosing his sheep."

No other power on earth has made such blasphemous claims or made such changes to God's law.

9. Daniel 7:25: It would rule 1260 years. This is a most dramatic prophecy! In A.D. 538 papal Rome finally destroyed the Ostrogoths. Emperor Justinian gave the kingdom over to the Bishop of Rome that year. Add 1260 years to that, and you come to 1798, the year of the French Revolution. In 1798 Napoleon's armies overthrew the papal power, confiscated all the property of the kingdom, declared a republic, and took the pope off the throne, where in France, he died in exile. Exactly 1260 years as prophesied!

Now that the Bible has clearly established the identity of the little horn/kingdom in Daniel 7, let's go to the beast kingdom of Revelation 13 and notice the similarities. In Revelation 13, the beast who speaks great words and blasphemy also rules 42 months, which equals 1260 days. In Revelation 13:7 it also makes war with God's people. Revelation 13:3 says it receives a deadly wound. Comparing the little horn and the beast, we see that they are one and the same power. And it is this power that God says not to worship, nor to worship his image, nor to receive his mark.

In the foregoing, we have identified the beast, now we want to discover what the mark of the beast is.

When Jesus returns to this earth there will only be two groups of people on earth: the righteous and the wicked. As God brings this world of sin to an end, this distinction will come about as the result of a specific issue. This issue causes all people to make a decision as to which side they will be on. That issue revolves around a decision: Will we worship the beast, his image, and receive the mark of the beast? Or will we worship God, follow His truth and receive the seal of God? Revelation 14:9, 10 gives this warning:

> **"And the third angel followed them, saying with a loud voice, If any man *worship the beast* and *his image*, and receive *his mark* in his forehead, or in his hand, The same shall drink of the wine of the wrath of God, which is poured out without mixture into the cup of his indignation; and he shall be tormented with fire and brimstone in the presence of the holy angels, and in the presence of the Lamb."**—emphasis supplied.

In Revelation 15:1 we're told the wrath of God is the seven last plagues just before Jesus comes. These plagues will be the most terrible scourges ever poured out upon man. Now let's ask an important question: Would our God, who is so determined to save us, threaten us with this terrible wrath *if we couldn't know who the beast is, and what his mark is?* No! Thus, in His word, God has made it abundantly clear who the beast is—as we have already seen—and what the mark of the beast will be.

The Bible teaches that only those who have the seal of God are saved (Revelation 7:2, 3). God will give each person the opportunity to choose whether they will yield their allegiance to Him or to the beast power. So whatever the mark of the beast is, it is obviously something about which God feels very strongly.

Notice that the beast of Revelation 13 is made up of the four beasts of Daniel 7. It has the body of the *leopard*, feet of the *bear*, mouth of the *lion*, and the ten horns of the fourth beast. Why is it thus depicted? It is because the papal system incorporated doctrines, beliefs, practices, and teachings from all these pagan empires, especially Babylon. It clothed these false teachings in a spiritual garb and spread them to the whole world.

God is calling His people out of Babylon:

> **"And he cried mightily with a strong voice, saying, Babylon the great is fallen, is fallen, and is become the habitation of devils, and the hold of every foul spirit, and a cage of every unclean and hateful bird. For all nations have drunk of the wine of the wrath of her fornication, and the kings of the earth have committed fornication with her, and the merchants of the earth are waxed rich through the abundance of her delicacies. And I heard another voice from heave, saying, *Come out of her, my people, that ye be not partakers of her sins, and the ye receive not of her plagues.*"**—Revelation 18:2, 3, emphasis supplied.

Come out, *my* people, God says! God longs for His people in Babylon to leave behind its twisted theology and become part of God's commandment-keeping people who have the faith of Jesus!

In Revelation 14:9, 10 God describes those who worship the beast:

> **"And the third angel followed them, saying with a loud voice, If any man worship the beast and his image, and receive his mark in his forehead, or in his hand, The same shall drink of the wine of the wrath of God, which is poured out without mixture into the cup of his indignation; and he shall be tormented with fire and brimstone in the presence of the holy angels, and in the presence of the Lamb."**

However, in verse 12 he describes the saints who stand in contrast as those who "keep the commandments of God":

> **"Here is the patience of the saints: here are they that *keep the commandments of God,* and the faith of Jesus."**—emphasis supplied.

This is repeated several times:

> **"And the dragon was wroth with the woman, and went to make war with the remnant of her seed, which *keep the commandments of God,* and have the testimony of Jesus Christ."**—Revelation 12:17, emphasis supplied.

> **"Blessed are they that *do his commandments,* that they may have right to the tree of life, and may enter in through the gates into the city."**—Revelation 22:14, emphasis supplied.

But then Revelation gives another identifying mark of God's people in the last days:

> **"And I saw another angel ascending from the east, having the seal of the living God: and he cried with a loud voice to the four angels, to whom it was given to hurt the earth and the sea, Saying, Hurt not the earth, neither the sea, nor the trees, till we have *sealed* the servants of our God in their foreheads."**—Revelation 7:2, 3, emphasis supplied.

God's servants thus will have the "seal of God" in their foreheads. What is the seal of God? Revelation 22:4 says it is the Father's name in their forehead. "And they shall see his face; and *his name* shall be in their foreheads." This is repeated in Revelation 14:1: "And I looked, and, lo, a Lamb stood on the mount Sion, and with him an hundred forty and four thousand, having *his Father's name written in their foreheads*" (emphasis supplied).

This is crucial to see, for notice how the mark of the beast is described.

Revelation 14:11 says it is the "mark of his name" in their foreheads. "And the smoke of their torment ascendeth up for ever and ever: and they have no rest day nor night, who worship the beast and his image, and whosoever receiveth the *mark of his name*" (emphasis supplied). So the issue the world is facing boils down to these two sides with two marks distinguishing between them.

We noted in chapter 4 of this book (*Jerusalem Caliphate and the Third Jihad*) that the seal of God was found in the fourth commandment. We saw that the seal of God had to do with the seventh-day Sabbath.

This *seal* is almost certainly not a literal, visible seal that will be stamped into believers' foreheads but rather is a settling into the truth of God, a decision to follow Jesus. Your forehead represents your mind, where you make decisions. When you choose God, His name and law is symbolically written in your mind. As Hebrews 10:15, 16 says: "Whereof the Holy Ghost also is a witness to us: for after that he had said before, This is the covenant that I will make with them after those days, saith the Lord, I will put my laws into their hearts, and *in their minds* will I write them" (emphasis supplied).

Now that we know what the seal of God is, what is the mark of the beast? Well, it's a simple step by step counterfeit of the seal of God! Let's turn back to the prophecy in Daniel 7:25:

> **"And he shall speak great words against the most High, and shall wear out the saints of the most High, and *think to change times and laws*: and they shall be given into his hand until a time and times and the dividing of time."**—emphasis supplied.

Notice that the beast power changes *times*. Only the fourth commandment of the law deals with *times*—and indeed, it is a prime example of how the Roman Church has attempted to change God's times and laws. Note what *The Convert's Catechism of Catholic Doctrine*, by Reverend Peter Geirmann, has to say:

"Q. Which is the Sabbath day?

A. Saturday is the Sabbath day.

Q. Why do we observe Sunday instead of Saturday?

A. We observe Sunday instead of Saturday because the Catholic Church, in the Council of Laodicea (A.D. 336) transferred the solemnity from Saturday to Sunday."

As these changes were made, papal Rome began to spread these teachings throughout the world that it ruled. The Bible writers had already foreseen this and had already begun to warn us about it:

> **"And every spirit that confesseth not that Jesus Christ is come in the flesh is not of God: and this is that spirit of antichrist, whereof ye have heard that it should come; and even now already is it in the world."**—1 John 4:3.

John said the spirit of antichrist is already working in the world in his day! Then Paul in 2 Thessalonians 2:3, 4, 7, speaking of later developments of the antichrist, wrote these words:

> **"Let no man deceive you by any means: for that day shall not come, except there come falling away first, and that man of sin be revealed, the son of perdition; Who opposeth and exalteth himself above all that is *called God*, or *that is worshipped*; so that he as God sitteth in the temple of God, shewing himself that *he is God*. For the mystery of iniquity doth *already work*: only he who now letteth will let, until he be taken out of the way."**—emphasis supplied.

As we continue through history, we find that people began to protest the actions of the Roman Church in twisting the Word of God. This eventually started what we now call the Protestant Reformation. As the Reformation grew and the authority of the Bible began to challenge the authority of the papal Church, the papacy was faced with widespread opposition. In the 1500s, the decision was made to put tradition ahead of the Bible, based on the "fact" that the Church had power to do so, since it was God on earth, and had indeed found widespread success in "changing" God's law and the Sabbath day of worship. Notice these quotes:

> "The Archbishop of Reggio made a speech in which he openly declared that tradition stood above Scriptures.... The church had changed.... Sabbath into Sunday, not by the command of Christ, but by its own authority."—*Canon and Tradition*, by Holtzmann, p. 263.

Notice that the archbishop claimed that the very basis of papal authority was founded upon the change of the Sabbath to Sunday.

> "The church is above the Bible and this transference of Sabbath to Sunday is proof of that fact."—*Catholic Record*, September 1, 1923.

> "Of course the Catholic church claims that the change was her act. And the act is the *mark* of her ecclesiastical power and authority in religious matters."—*Faith of Our Fathers*, p. 14, C.F. Thomas, Chancellor of Cardinal Gibbons, emphasis supplied.

The Protestant churches, by honoring Sunday as the Sabbath in place of the seventh-day Sabbath are unwittingly accepting the authority of the Catholic Church as noted by the following statements:

"Reason and sense demand the acceptance of one or the other of these alternatives: either Protestantism and the keeping holy of Saturday, or Catholicity and the keeping holy of Sunday. Compromise is impossible."—John Cardinal Gibbons, *The Catholic Mirror*, December 23, 1893.

"The Sabbath was Saturday, not Sunday. The Church altered the observance of the Sabbath to the observance of Sunday. Protestants must be rather puzzled by the keeping of Sunday when God distinctly said, 'Keep holy the Sabbath Day.' The word Sunday does not come anywhere in the Bible, so, without knowing it they are obeying the authority of the Catholic Church."—*Canon Cafferata, The Catechism Explained*, p. 89.

"It is well to remind the Presbyterians, Baptists, Methodists, and all other Christians, that the Bible does not support them anywhere in their observance of Sunday. Sunday is an institution of the Roman Catholic Church, and those who observe the day observe a commandment of the Catholic Church." Priest Brady, in an address, reported in the Elizabeth, NJ 'News' on March 18, 1903.

"Protestants...accept Sunday rather than Saturday as the day for public worship after the Catholic Church made the change... But the Protestant mind does not seem to realize that...in observing Sunday, they are accepting the authority of the spokesman for the Church, the Pope."—*Our Sunday Visitor*, February 5, 1950.

The fact that most Protestants churches honor Sunday as the day of worship—a change that was made by the beast—has prophetic significance:

The papacy is portrayed by another symbol in Revelation—the woman of Revelation 17 who is described as "the great whore that sitteth upon many waters"—Revelation 17:1. Notice that this woman is the mother of harlots. In other words, she has daughters:

"And upon her forehead was a name written, MYSTERY, BABYLON THE GREAT, THE MOTHER OF HARLOTS AND ABOMINATIONS OF THE EARTH."—Revelation 17:5.

These harlot daughters would be made in the image of their mother. The fact that most Protestants churches accept and promote the very day of worship that the mother/beast set up in direct violation of the fourth commandment makes them faithful daughters of their mother. These daughters play a prominent role in connection with the two-horned beast of Revelation 13:

> **"And I beheld another beast coming up out of the earth; and he had two horns like a lamb, and he spake as a dragon. And he exerciseth all the power of the first beast before him, and causeth the earth and them which dwell therein to worship the first beast, whose deadly wound was healed."**—Revelation 13:11, 12.

"The lamblike horns indicate youth, innocence, and gentleness, fitly representing the character of the United States when presented to the prophet as 'coming up' in 1798. Among the Christian exiles who first fled to America and sought an asylum from royal oppression and priestly intolerance were many who determined to establish a government upon the broad foundation of *civil and religious liberty* [two lamblike horns]. Their views found place in the Declaration of Independence, which sets forth the great truth that 'all men are created equal' and endowed with the inalienable right to 'life, liberty, and the pursuit of happiness.' And the Constitution guarantees to the people the right of self-government, providing that representatives elected by the popular vote shall enact and administer the laws. Freedom of religious faith was also granted, every man being permitted to worship God according to the dictates of his conscience. *Republicanism and Protestantism* became the fundamental principles of the nation. These principles are the secret of its power and prosperity."—*The Great Controversy*, 441, emphasis supplied.

Lamblike horns, yet it will speak as a dragon? These two horns have been worn down to stubs. We are beginning to hear the voice of the dragon as our constitutional rights are being eroded away.

When Protestant America enforces Sunday laws by congressional legislation, they will by this act form an image to the beast (Revelation 14:9). And it is only when this final test—regarding loyalty to the commandments of God (seventh-day Sabbath) versus loyalty to the commandments of the beast (Sunday)—takes place that anyone will be found worshiping the beast and his image and receiving his mark.

For more information on these prophecies see chapter 25 of *The Great Controversy* and read the commentary on Revelation 13 in *Daniel and the Revelation*—these two books can be downloaded for free at daniel1145. com under the "Books" tab.

ASSURANCE DEFINED

What Is the Faith of Jesus?

Consider the faith of Jesus for a moment. For Jesus to have been "in all points tempted like as we are. . ." (Heb. 4:15), the possibility of yielding to sin had to have been there. Jesus knew that His life of continual obedience would be possible only if He continued to submit moment by moment to His Father's will. He also knew that His resurrection as our Redeemer would be based upon the condition that He remain victorious.

Such was His understanding of the conditions; but what was His faith? "Jesus said unto them, The Son of man shall be betrayed into the hands of men: and they shall kill him, and the third day he shall be raised again." (Matthew 17:22, 23). Jesus spoke confidently of His resurrection, indicating that He had faith that His father would keep Him from yielding to sin. Did Jesus have any Word from God that He could place His faith in that declared that He would remain victorious until the end? He found that Word in Isaiah 42:4: "He shall not fail nor be discouraged, till he have set judgment in the earth . . ." He even had a promise regarding His resurrection: "For thou wilt not leave my soul in hell; neither wilt thou suffer thine Holy One to see corruption." (Psalms 16:10).

Do we have any Word from God that we can place our faith in which will give us hope that God will keep us from falling? Can we believe this with the same assurance with which Jesus believed? Yes, indeed! "And the Lord shall deliver me from every evil work, and will preserve me unto his heavenly kingdom: to whom be glory for ever and ever. Amen." (2 Timothy 4:18). "Now unto him that is able to keep you from falling." (Jude 1:24).

Faith is expecting the Word of God itself to do what that Word says, and depending upon that Word alone to accomplish what it declares. Jesus lived by every Word that proceeded out of the mouth of God. He put His faith in God's Word, expecting the Word to accomplish what it said. And according to His faith, it was unto Him (Matt. 9:29). This is the faith of Jesus, and it is by this the Christian lives. "And the life I now live, I live by the faith *of* the son of God who loved me and gave himself for me." (Galatians 2:20).

A correct understanding of theological facts is important, but, "this is the victory that overcometh the world, even our faith." (1 John 5:4). Jesus had faith in the written Word and declared with David, "I have inclined my heart to perform thy statutes always, even unto the end." (Psalms 119:12). God's Word has creative power, and Jesus' faith in the Word caused it to be true in His life. That Word also says, "O bless our God ... which holdeth our soul in life, and suffereth not our feet to be moved." (Psalms 66:8, 9). Jesus believed that His soul would be held in life, and according to His faith, it was unto Him.

It came to me as a new thought to believe that my soul would be held in life. I had not realized that we have a right to say, "The Lord shall deliver me from every evil work." (2 Timothy 4:18). My history of being overcome in temptation made it seem impossible for me to believe that I would not continue to fail. My only option to faith was to deny the promise of God by unbelief.

Are you living by the faith of the Son of God? If so, you too should be able to say, "I have set the Lord always before me, because He is at my right hand, I shall not be moved." (Psalms 16:8). The faith of Jesus is simply believing every promise that proceeds out of the mouth of God.